Praise for *Soul*

"In *Soul Excavation* Lesia Kohut tells us that in order to truly heal trauma and wounds of the past we must activate our soul; we must reconnect with our divinity and take responsibility for the life we have created for ourselves.

Offering spiritual insights and principles through a quantum lens, Lesia demonstrates how we can consciously choose to stop being bound by our past and ultimately awaken to how infinitely powerful, creative, and resilient we truly are. As we awaken and heal ourselves, we heal the soul of the world.

Lesia's writing style is entertaining and easy to understand, and I have no doubt that many will see themselves in and be inspired by the stories and quantum realizations shared in this book. *Soul Excavation* truly deserves to be widely read. Read this book!"

– Paul Levy, author of *Wetiko: Healing the Mind-Virus that Plagues Our World*, *The Quantum Revelation: A Radical Synthesis of Science and Spirituality,* and *Dispelling Wetiko: Breaking the Curse of Evil*

* * *

"Lesia Kohut has a deep and sparkling outlook on her life. But best of all she has wit and intelligence. She has many voices speaking to her and guiding her, and so her simple but lively words will help you find your way. She is not dogmatic, but she is serious in her search for what I would call her soul. You will enjoy reading this book and learn how to dig into your life and your world for their infinite richness."

– Thomas Moore, author of *Care of the Soul*

* * *

"Lesia Kohut is a poet. Her words evoke the sense that All is Well, no matter who you are or what you are currently experiencing in life. Her story is one discovering the Truth that lies in the center of every living being: we are in God, and God is in us. Buttressed by her intricate and detailed study of those who have taught spiritual Truth, she describes her own awakening and bids us all to take the journey for ourselves.

The "About This Book" section also has some of the most organized, easy-to-read information explaining some of the basic principles of New Thought, including what happens during soul retrieval. Read this book!"

– Maria Nemeth, Ph.D., author of *Mastering Life's Energies* and *The Energy of Money*

* * *

"In this amazingly raw, real, and revealing book, Lesia lays it all on the table. Her ability, vulner-ability and mastery of sharing her life story had me look deeply into the beliefs, stories, and dimensions of my life that were both enlightening and confronting. And I dare say, that is the job of this book. I found myself awash in her stories and reflecting profoundly at the same time about the origins and desires of my own life. Lesia had me "feel the quantum field," not just read about it. And I believe, when we experience this at a deep level, we are then truly free to create whatever we long to experience with the amazing gift called "our lives." Thank you Lesia for your gift to us to have us really know who we are at our core...soul creative beings! Your words touched me at a level that opened me up to real possibility. I know they will for many others as well. Forever grateful!"

– Rick Tamlyn, Hay House author of Play Your Bigger Game

* * *

"I hope many come to meet Lesia Kohut and read *Soul Excavation*. And part of what she said in two short sentences so reminded me of my own work with some of the greats like Rumi & Hafiz. Lesia said, "I believe words can be limiting. And I believe words can be liberating."

Indeed, the beauty, truth and wonderful power in some words can so help unfurl the golden wing inside, and let us caress more and more of the sun – a precious light we so need to know that is in the heart of all things."

– Daniel Ladinsky, International Bestselling Penguin Author

Soul Excavation

An Exploration and Discovery of Self
Through Fear, Failure, and
Quantum Physics

by Lesia Daria Kohut

Published by
Hybrid Global Publishing
333 E 14th Street
#3C
New York, NY 10003

Manufactured in the United States of America, or in the United Kingdom when distributed elsewhere.

Kohut, Lesia.
Soul Excavation
   ISBN: 978-1-957013-25-1 (paperback)
   ISBN: 978-1-957013-63-3 (hardcover)
   eBook: 978-1-957013-26-8
   LCCN: 2022905270

Cover design by: Jonathan Pleska
Copyediting by: Wendie Pecharsky
Interior design by: Suba Murugan
Author's Photo by: Linda Mackie

Infinite love and gratitude expressed for the following permissions from previously published works:

Excerpts from Care of the Soul by Thomas Moore. Copyright © 1992 by Thomas Moore. Used by permission of HarperCollins Publishers.

Excerpts from Care of the Soul by Thomas Moore.Copyright © 1992 by Thomas Moore. Reproduced with permission of the Little Brown Group Limited through PLSclear.

"When the Violin," from the Penguin publication A Year With Hafiz: Daily Contemplations by Daniel Ladinsky, copyright 2011 and used with permission.

Excerpts from The Alchemist by Paulo Coelho. Copyright © 1988 by Paulo Coelho. English translation copyright © 1993 by Paulo Coelho and Alan R. Clarke. Use by permission of HarperCollins Publishers.

Excerpts from The Alchemist by Paulo Coelho. Reprinted by permission of HarperCollins Publishers Ltd © 1988 by Paulo Coelho.

Excerpt from SEVEN THOUSAND WAYS TO LISTEN: Staying Close to What Is Sacred by Mark Nepo. Copyright © 2012 by Mark Nepo. Reprinted with the permission of Atria Books, a division of Simon & Schuster, Inc. All rights reserved.

Excerpts from pages 93, 150, 173, 183, 217, and 261 from the Select Books publication The Quantum Revelation: A Radical Synthesis of Science and Spirituality by Paul Levy. Copyright 2018 by Paul Levy. Used with the author's permission.

Excerpt from THE ENERGY CODES by Dr. Sue Morter. Copyright 2019 by Dr. Sue Morter. Reprinted with permission of Atria Books, a Division of Simon & Schuster, Inc. All rights reserved.

Excerpt(s) from RUMI by Rumi, translated by Jonathan Star, copyright © 1997 by Jonathan Star. Used by permission of Tarcher, an imprint of Penguin Publishing Group, a division of Penguin. Random House LLC. All rights reserved.

www.lesiakohut.com

For my dad.

Contents

Contents

Soul Excavation (n.)/ the mindful, messy, and dynamic work of digging through and unearthing the limiting thoughts, stories, and beliefs that keep us feeling stuck; revealing life's most extraordinary treasure—the Infinite Creativity, Resilience, and Love we truly are.

Foreword

by
Dr. James Mellon, founding spiritual director of
the Global Truth Center Los Angeles, author of
Mental Muscle and *The Five Questions*

There are students that come along and question the very ground you walk on. They are smart and quick and filled with learned answers they've spent a lifetime cultivating. Such a student is a wonderous breath of fresh air, filling the room with possibility and all the while keeping an eye on anything that might need rescripting. This type of student is the type I most enjoy. They challenge me, question me, expand me, and in the end inhabit the journey in such a way as to benefit us both. This is who Lesia Kohut was and is to me.

The book you have before you is witness to the life of a young woman with a challenging youth, a rocky adolescence, and numerous opportunities to overcome, understand, and create anew. Lesia Kohut takes us on a journey into her world, and not only describes in achingly honest terms the history that is her life, but also illuminates the entire landscape with a rich perspective on what it means to be human in the spiritual sense. She has a no-nonsense approach to writing that is refreshing, audacious, and at the same time loving and respectful.

It's one thing to remember our childhood, it's quite another to have a perspective that helps us live with what was by examining what is and all the while knowing what can be. This is the particular gift of Lesia Kohut. In *Soul Excavation* she does not shy away from the relative facts of her life, but she also does not dwell in the emotional shadows of what was. She understands the philosophy she has trained in and uses it to make sense, spiritual sense, out of it all. Her point of view is healthy and vital and allows us, the reader, to see ourselves in the process.

It has been an honor to be a part of Lesia's journey thus far. She is an important mind in a world that needs as many of us as are willing to stay the course of living from and as love. I believe this book puts an impactful dosage of love into the world and we all benefit from it. Thank you, Lesia, and thank you, dear reader, for taking this journey. We're all in this together.

About This Book

For nearly twelve years, I've wanted to write a book. And for nearly twelve years, I've talked about writing a book. In fact, if I'd written a book every time I'd talked about it, I probably would've written about ten books on ten different topics by now. However, over the years, instead of writing, I'd end up getting distracted by something shinier—work, life, school—and that shininess received my attention instead.

Until this time. *This time*, it was different.

On the outside, the reason for writing this book was quite simple. It was the final requirement for a bachelor's degree in advanced consciousness studies granted through the Emerson Theological Institute. Submit the book, get my degree. No book, no degree.

On the inside, however, it was a bit more complex. In fact, it really meant having to consider why it had taken over twelve years to write this first book. Or rather, why for the twelve years I'd talked about writing a book, I hadn't produced even one.

I'd had the desire. I had plenty of material. And some might even argue, I had the talent. But there was always something that got in the way. There was always something that held me back. The list of reasons—excuses, really—seemed endless:

- *The book I was about to start writing is already changing, so I'll just wait until I gather enough material for this new idea.*
- *There are already so many self-help books out there, why should I add mine to the list?*
- *I don't have the time, energy, or money to write the book I want to write.*
- *I don't have the time, energy, or money to write the book people will want to buy.*
- *No one knows who I am, so why would they buy my book over someone else's who's famous?*
- *I don't know how.*
- *I don't know where to start.*

Looking at that list today, although many reasons can still sound somewhat compelling, I view that list with a very different set of eyes. When I look at that list now, I see beyond the reasons, beyond the excuses. What I see, are beliefs. Beliefs of, "You're not good enough," "You're not smart enough," and "You don't have what it takes."

And that's what this book is about.

It's about the three main stories in my life that illustrate the deep-rooted beliefs that kept me feeling stuck in pain, anger, and fear for most of my life. Beliefs that literally got in the way of me doing anything that felt even remotely uncomfortable or could change the status quo.

These beliefs were the foundation for every decision I made, every relationship I had, and whether or not my life was even worth living.

It's about identifying so profoundly with failure and shame, that I actually believed failure and shame were who I was. It's about how I thought if people got too close to me, they might catch or become infected with my brokenness.

However, this book is also about something bigger. Thanks to my five years of intensive spiritual/consciousness studies, it's about what I've come to understand—at least in part—and know myself to be. It's what poets, mystics, philosophers, artists, metaphysicians, and quantum physicists endeavour to write and paint about and study. It's about that one Universal Energy that is the very essence, activity, and interconnectivity of everyone and everything. Call it God, call it the Universe, call it Love. It's who and what each and every one of us is at our core.

Ultimately, this book is about how there is nothing that we could ever think, believe, feel, or experience that will ever stop this infinite creativity and resilience from bubbling its way to the surface. It's meant to bubble up and out. And we're meant to live our lives from and as that extraordinary creativity, resilience, and love.

Do I have life all figured out? No. Am I a work in progress? Absolutely. Even during the writing of this book I'd find myself surprised time and time again at the thoughts, beliefs, and feelings that would percolate gently or violently erupt, leaving me feeling anywhere from mildly affected to completely emotionally exhausted for days. Even though I had worked through everything I've written about in the following chapters, there were still new ways of looking at my life, of honouring the old thoughts, beliefs, and feelings, and the people and circumstances that have all brought me here, to this now moment.

I suspect some of what I share might resonate with others. Perhaps it will open a window or doorway to a new way of thinking, believing, or feeling that just because life has looked a certain way up until now, doesn't mean it has to look the same going forward.

Because my spiritual/consciousness studies have been the main impetus for this exploration into self, there are certain terms I use throughout the book which may not be familiar to some. I have endeavoured to explain things as plainly as possible throughout the book, but just for good measure, here are a few key terms that could do with a little extra explanation:

- **Activational** – a state of being so fully inspired that we are impelled into immediate action, allowing us to more easily attract answers to questions we may have, and resources we may require, as we realize our intended goal.
- **Quantum field** – A more scientific term for God; the field where everything is possible. This is the never-ending buffet of possibilities we are constantly choosing from with our minds—knowingly or unknowingly. In this realm things are waves of possibility, or particles of actuality. Every time we choose a possibility by placing our attention on it, it becomes our actual life experience. That experience is shaped by our

tendency of thought (our habitual thought patterns), along with the prominent beliefs and feelings that are in play—whether we're aware of them or not.

- **Religious science practitioner/Licensed spiritual practitioner** – Someone who has undergone and passed the required four years of intensive, immersive study and training as required by either the Emerson Theological Institute or the Holmes Institute for Consciousness Studies. A practitioner is skilled in performing Spiritual Mind Treatment and in supporting clients in shifting from identifying with their problems to embracing and embodying a more desirable, empowered way of living.

- **Science of Mind** – A teaching philosophy, book, and way of life written and realized by Ernest Holmes. The three main tenets of this teaching philosophy are:

  * **There is only one thing going on.** Call it God, the Universe, Energy, Love, or the quantum field—whatever is meaningful for you. It is the very essence of everyone and everything. It is infinite in scope (boundless, limitless, eternal), and creative by nature (it's always shifting, changing, evolving, and expanding).

  * **Everyone and everything is that one thing.** In other words, we are all walking, talking, living, breathing, unique, original expressions of Infinite Creative Energy. This includes tangible things like people, places, and things. It also includes intangible things like thoughts, beliefs, and feelings. God is all there is. Energy is all there is. There is nothing that isn't God. There is nothing that isn't Energy.

- * **We live according to spiritual and natural laws, with the main law being the law of cause and effect.** From a scientific perspective, you kick a ball, it moves. You kick a wall, either the wall is dented, or your foot breaks. From a spiritual perspective, what you think, believe, and feel becomes the foundation for your life experience.

- **Soul Excavation** – The mindful, messy, and dynamic work of digging through and unearthing the limiting thoughts, stories, and beliefs that keep us feeling stuck; revealing life's most extraordinary treasure—the Infinite Creativity, Resilience, and Love we truly are.

- **Spiritual/Consciousness Studies** –
  - * Two years of foundational classes on spirituality, philosophy, metaphysics, meditation, Spiritual Mind Treatment (also known as Affirmative Prayer), and history of the New Thought movement.
  - * The two-year comprehensive, life-altering Spiritual Practitioner Studies program following foundational classes. This is the program through which I became licensed as a religious science practitioner, accredited by the Emerson Theological Institute.
  - * One year of Advanced Consciousness Studies—The first class of its kind, developed and facilitated by Dr. James Mellon, founder and spiritual director of the Global Truth Center Los Angeles, in conjunction with the Emerson Theological Institute. This class was an engaging, mind-blowing exploration and inquiry into the meaning of *Consciousness*.

- **Spiritual Mind Treatment** – An activational technique also known as Affirmative Prayer that argues for the truth beyond immediate circumstances—no matter what is going on. It is the main tool used by spiritual practitioners to consciously move energy (or shift the practitioner's mindset) for a specific purpose. It is performed using words or in silence, with the practitioner going through a series of steps which include:
  * **Recognizing** there is only God/Energy/Love.
  * **Identifying**—with every fibre of one's being—as God/Energy/Love, and knowing the same for everyone and everything, including our client.
  * **Declaring** or **realizing** the specific intention of the Treatment/Prayer. It is all done in the present tense, using only positive, affirmative language (we don't bring the problem into the Treatment). There is no wishing or hoping here. We are knowing the truth and infinite potentiality of the situation. We are tapping into and drawing from the completed vision of our intention.
  * Expressing **gratitude**, knowing the Treatment/Prayer is already a successful done deal and that our intention is fully realized and fully orbed—right here, right now.
  * **Releasing** any attachment to outcome, knowing that God/Energy/Love is doing its thing, working its magic, and taking care of the *how* now that we've been clear on the *what* of our intention. This is about Trust, Faith, and moving forward with life from a new, higher level of Consciousness or awareness and acceptance (a more positive, life-affirming mindset), rather than going back to focusing on the problem and constantly wondering, "Is it done yet?"

This book is also laid out in a way that shows the trajectory or arc from where I was to where I am in this moment. The sections of the book also correspond to the Soul Excavation process.

The first section begins—as does the Excavation—with digging into the past (stories). Writing this book has been my opportunity to mindfully, compassionately, and sometimes messily revisit the three main stories that have had the most profound impact on how I've lived most of my life so far.

The second section corresponds to the next phase of this work. It's about unearthing and becoming aware of the ideas that we've mistaken for truths (beliefs) that have been the foundation from which we've lived our life so far. It's about understanding the impact those beliefs have had. It's also about realizing and embracing new beliefs that are more supportive and life-affirming. More specifically, this section of the book is about the beliefs that had been my foundation for most of my life, and how I eventually came to realize that not only were they not true, but most of them weren't even mine.

The third section and subsequent phase of the work is about discovery (treasure). It's about the buried truth of the Infinite Creativity, Resilience, and Love we've been all along. It's also about the wisdom and insights brought to light along the way to not only rediscovering Who and What we are, but to living from and as that Infinite Creativity in action. This section is about how the first two phases of Soul Excavation eventually led me to discovering the Infinite Creativity, Resilience, and Love that I am and have been all along.

Finally, even though there is an overall progression, sometimes we can jump from one phase to another—seemingly out of order—while at other times, we can be immersed in more than one phase at the same time. At least that's how it's been for me.

So here it is. My final assignment for my degree. My thoughtful, insightful, compassionate labour of self-love.

It's taken me over twelve years to write this first book and I'm still uncovering the stuff of which I am made. I am infinitely grateful for every moment it has taken me to shift from living from pain, anger, and fear to living *as* the Infinite Creativity, Resilience, and Love I now know myself to be.

I am equally grateful for your time and presence and for everything that comes next.

With infinite love and gratitude,

When the Violin

Hafiz by Daniel Ladinsky

When the violin can forgive the past it
starts singing.

When the violin can stop worrying
about the future

you will become such a drunk laughing
nuisance

the Sun will then lean down and start
combing you into its hair.

When the violin can forgive every wound
caused by others

your soul, your soul will start singing.

Introduction

"God is Love."

"God is Love."

"God is Love."

This is the statement my dad kept repeating in the days leading up to his death. At the time, although the word "God" and the statement itself got under my skin, I'd repeat it back to him because it seemed to bring him a great deal of comfort and peace of mind as he reconciled that—after two years of being convinced he was going to beat cancer—he was actually dying.

Seven years later, I wish I could talk to my dad about what that statement really meant to him. I wish I could talk to him about what that statement means to me now. I wish I could tell him in person, "Myroslave" (I always called my dad by his first name), "I get it now…God is love, and Love is all there is. It is Who and What I am. It is Who and What you are."

* * *

1

Growing up in Edmonton, Alberta, I had plenty of opportunity to experience God. Pretty much every Sunday my family went to church—to either St. Josaphat's Cathedral with my grandparents or St. George's Ukrainian Catholic Church with our parents. It was a formal affair, with us donning our Sunday best. When my sister and I were younger, that meant matching outfits with colour-coordinated sweaters, dresses, stockings, and shoes carefully and lovingly curated by my mom. A respectful sense of style and presentation were important—as much for God as for the community.

Before we entered the church, we were reminded to be on our best behaviour. No talking. No fidgeting. No giggling under any circumstances. Church was serious business, and if we laughed or had a good time during the Divine Liturgy, we were going to hell.

From the moment we walked in the door, the iconography on the walls, the stained glass, the opulent robes worn by the clergy, and the hushed tones all lent themselves to the palpable reverence of faith by all who were there. The candles, incense, ritual, and music all added to the richness of the sacred experience of being in church, reminding us that we were in the presence of God.

Much of the time, though, I had no idea what the priests were saying because they spoke so quickly, with their eyes closed as if in a trance, uttering an ancient, mystical language that only they and God could understand. A great deal of the Divine Liturgy would also take place from behind the *iconostas*—in Ukrainian churches, the barrier separating the nave from the sanctuary. The iconostas was decorated beautifully, extravagantly, and in great detail, with various icons and religious imagery. Saints, apostles, vignettes of pivotal moments in Jesus's life, death, and resurrection. All of these elements added extra layers of mystique to my fascinating church-going experience.

From around the age of eight, as soon as we'd arrive, I'd find a prayer book and song book and follow along. I'd respond on cue with the appropriate response, prayer, or song, standing, sitting, or kneeling as was required, as was respectful. It felt so important to be part of something that was steeped in so much ritual and reverence and to be so interconnected with the community and with the mysterious, all-powerful God.

I also remember spending lots of time looking at all of the iconography and artistry that graced every square inch of St. Josaphat's Cathedral. It was common knowledge that the artist who'd painted the inside of the cathedral had used faces of people in the community as references for many of the characters that made up Jesus's life story.

I remember how my sister and I would delight in recognizing the faces of family and community members forever immortalized as an angel, a villager, an apostle, one of the unfortunate cast into hell, or some other relevant character. We loved seeing two of my mom's cousins—who happened to be sisters and favourite aunts of ours—as angels, gracefully gazing at us from one of the walls closest to our pew.

One of the most interesting faces in the church for me was that of God. I remember looking up at the ceiling of the main dome so many times, and there he was. Larger than life, with fiery hair and a beard that felt alive; eyes that told you they knew *everything* you'd been up to and were even thinking about. And every time

I looked at that image, I'd wonder, *Why is God so angry? If God loves everyone and everything unconditionally and wants the best for us all... why does he look so angry?*

Now, I was a little kid, and it was an artist's interpretation of God. In fact, I eventually learned the face of God was actually the face of the artist who'd painted the church. However, from everything I'd understood from church, Ukrainian school, hearing my family talk about God and Christianity, and being Ukrainian, the idea of God was confusing to me. Belief in God was a *huge* part of Ukrainian culture, and I loved the idea of being Ukrainian Catholic. To me, it meant being part of a community—of culture, artistry, and ritual. The idea of God, though, didn't always make sense.

We were told God was everywhere, and that I was either made in the image of God or was a part of God. If God were indeed everywhere, wouldn't that mean that God was not only in me, or a part of me, but that I actually *was* my own unique version of God? Again, to me, it didn't quite make sense.

God was also supposed to love unconditionally. Well, if that was true, what was hell all about? What were all of these prayers we were meant to recite after weekly confession, after all of our weeklong sinning? Why did we even need to pray? If God loved unconditionally and was everywhere, wouldn't he just know love for us no matter what? And who were these men—there were no women priests, just men—who told us what and how often to pray?

And what about all the horrible stuff in the world: war, poverty, disease, murder, and harm that seemed to be on the

4

news so often? How could a loving God allow for all of that to happen—to me, my family, my friends, and people throughout the world?

Even with all of those questions, there was still a part of me that loved the idea of God and religion so much that when I was a little girl, I actually wanted to be a priest—a Ukrainian Catholic priest. Yet, when I told my Ukrainian school religion teacher—an elderly Ukrainian Orthodox priest adored by many—he gently smiled at me and said, "I'm sorry Lesia, but you can never be a priest because you're a girl."

Talk about having my dreams crushed! What did my being a girl have anything to do with anything? What did it matter that I wasn't a boy who'd grow up to be a man? Did it mean that in God's eyes, I didn't have what it'd take to serve God in such a profound way? Did it mean that because I was a girl, I was I somehow less capable of kindness, love, and compassion? I began to wonder whether perhaps God considered me not good enough or smart enough, and that I didn't have what it'd take to be of sacred service— because I was a girl.

During my early teens, still curious but also slightly jaded, I remember getting into several heated conversations about religion and faith with my dad. I remember him saying that faith was only part of it, and that deed was just as important, if not more so. Confusion came into play once again because I remember plenty of times when my sister and I would beg our parents to take us to church some Sundays, even though they really wanted, and ultimately opted, to sleep in. On the weekends, we slept over at my grandparents' house. For them, there was no excuse for not going to church. You went or you were going to hell. Did this mean my parents were going to hell?

And then there was confession. When I was younger, I was fascinated by it. I loved watching people as they lined up to go into the tiny wooden confessional so they could disclose their sins to the "on duty" priest. I loved it even more when it was my turn to go.

The smell of the wood, the delicate woven screen, and the tiny sliding door that revealed a mysterious voice on the other side. There I'd sometimes be almost grasping at the faintest of sins so I had something to share, so I could be assigned some prayers, so I could then be forgiven, and start the week with a brand-spankin'-new clean slate. For me, there was something exhilarating about being so honest and forthright, about fessing up your worst secrets to God, and then having God (through the priest) basically saying, "It's all good."

As I got older, though, I became more cynical about confession. It was somewhat troublesome to think that someone could do horrible things throughout the week and then simply relay their stories to someone who worked for God, and after repeating the assigned prayers could be not only forgiven, but also absolved. It was like a "get out of jail free card" that seemed somewhat hypocritical because most of the people who confessed to something this week would show up the following Sunday with either the same or a new set of sins to be forgiven for and absolved of. It seemed to be an endless cycle of "Wash, rinse, repeat."

To top it all off, I don't ever remember seeing my dad go to confession. By the very nature of our tenuous, often volatile relationship—in my mind at least—there was plenty he could've confessed to. After all, wasn't confession one of the "deeds" he'd spoken so adamantly about during some of those heated discussions we'd had? Didn't God care that my dad didn't seem to be bothered about being honest regarding some of the stuff he'd done—during the week and over the years?

When it came to faith, that's where I really got bogged down. As I continued to question the idea of God, religion, and faith, I started to wonder, *Is there really a God?*

The more I questioned, the fewer answers there were. Ultimately, I decided I was an atheist, and I didn't believe in anything. When I proudly (more defiantly, really) announced this to my dad, he basically said, "You are *not* an atheist. You are Ukrainian, and as a Ukrainian, you believe in God. Besides, you're not even eighteen yet so you don't know what to think. Until you're eighteen, and you live under my roof, you'll believe what I believe."

Even if you have an ideal relationship with a parent—which I did not—what teenager wants to be told what to think? Better yet, what teenager wants to be given the "as long as you live under my roof" speech? Does that work on anyone? So, I dug my heels in further, decided atheism was for me, and as soon as I could get out of the house and out from under my father's roof, I would.

Over the next 30ish years, short of the phrase "Oh, my god!" the word "God" pretty much disappeared from my vocabulary. The word "religion" also grew its own charge, although I still deeply valued ritual, traditions, and liturgical music. I could also walk into almost any kind of church anywhere, and—especially if there was wood, stained glass, and candles—could immediately feel a deep sense of calm, peace, and tranquility. Interestingly enough, though, I usually preferred to sit in an empty church rather than attend a service. Once people got thrown into the mix, it was another experience altogether.

There were curious blips, however, like when I was about eight months pregnant. One day I was hit with the very profound, in-my-face question: *What faith is our baby going to be raised in?* I was almost panic-stricken and so surprised that it was even a "thing" for me.

After a very brief discussion with my husband, who'd periodically attended a Unity church in Toronto, we decided because religion was such a huge part of Ukrainian culture—and our baby was going to be raised as Ukrainian as could be—there would be a christening. Even though Glenn and I had both spent most of our adult lives in Toronto, we'd have the christening in Edmonton, where I grew up and where most of my family was. That's how strong and deep the pull of culture, community, and religion were for me. Even though I didn't actually believe in God the way I had when I was a young girl, this still felt like the right thing to do for our unborn child.

At some point in my adult life I realized I actually wasn't an atheist. Just by believing that God didn't exist, I actually believed in something—that God didn't exist. The more I wondered about life, though, the more I wondered about my part in it. It got harder and harder for me to not consider that there was something beyond me and my life experience. At some point, I began considering there was something more powerful, extraordinary—like on an

"I created the Universe with my powers" kind of scale—or at the very least more mysterious than I and worth looking into. I became much more focused on spirituality rather than organized religion.

The teachings of Wayne Dyer had a profound impact on me. His words and the way he spoke really made me think about what my thoughts and beliefs had to do with the kind of life I was living and that perhaps what I was experiencing wasn't all determined by some fiery-haired man in a long white robe, sitting on a cloud looking angry all the time. Maybe, just maybe, I had more authority over my life than I'd understood until now.

I also loved how Wayne Dyer spoke so mindfully and how he seemed to pull these brilliant, amazing quotes out of thin air. He made me want to read more, to learn more, to understand more. As I listened to and read more of his work, I was soon led to the teachings of Louise Hay, Bruce Lipton, David Hawkins, Michael Singer, and Eckart Tolle.

Then, when I came upon the Science of Mind philosophy and teachings by Ernest Holmes shortly thereafter, my mind was blown wide open. My mind and heart kept expanding as I read Thomas Troward (someone Wayne Dyer quoted often), Wallace Wattles, and Ralph Waldo Emerson (another Wayne Dyer favourite). As I began taking classes, I was introduced to the more contemporary wisdom of Mary Morrisey and Thomas Moore. And, even more recently, as I began to dip my toes into the infinite potentiality of the quantum sea, I welcomed and was inspired by the wisdom and insights of Joe Dispenza, Amit Goswami, Paul Levy, Lynne McTaggart, and Dr. Sue Morter.

Although every one of these extraordinarily brilliant authors and teachers spoke or speaks a slightly different language, ultimately, they are all saying pretty much the same thing. *We are infinitely more powerful, creative, and resilient than anything we could ever think, believe, or feel; than anything we could ever experience.*

As we focus our attention and intention on the infinite potentiality (or limitless opportunities) of the present moment, we are able to create whatever life we want—as that Infinite Potentiality, as God, as Love.

Just as in the Science of Mind philosophy, it wasn't so much about what I was thinking or what I was thinking about God. It became about how I was thinking—*as* God.

Now, several years into my spiritual/consciousness studies, I am enthusiastically immersed in advanced consciousness studies and quantum physics. As I dive deeper and deeper into the mind-bending, life-altering rabbit hole of the quantum realm, the context, meaning, and interpretation of God seems more fluid than ever.

What began for me as an automatic belief in something because that's what my family, community, and culture dictated so many years ago, has grown and evolved over the years. What was once something I loved and worshipped, became something I began to question and ultimately rail against and dismiss. And even after keeping it buried for so many years, at some point, the question of *What is God and what does God mean to me?* began to bubble up once again, inviting and opening me up to coming full circle to an ongoing mystical curiosity that so profoundly ignites my imagination. It is a calling that runs so deep within my soul it aches—a mystery whose pull is so extraordinarily strong and irresistible, I cannot help but give myself up to its beauty, brilliance, and wonder.

It's been seven years since my dad died. It's been seven years since I sat at his bedside, hearing him repeat, "God is Love" over and over again in those last few weeks that led to his death.

Today, I wish I could talk to my dad about what that statement really meant to him. I wish I could talk to him about what that statement means to me now. Seven years later, I wish I could tell him in person, "Myroslave, I get it now...God is Love. It is Who and What I am. It is Who and What you are. Love is all there is."

This book is about my spiritual journey so far. It's very much about my own Soul Excavation—the ongoing exploration and discovery of Who and What I am, and What I can become. However, it's also very much about my relationship with my dad. It's about fear, failure, and faith. It's about understanding, compassion, and forgiveness. And in a very profound, tender, and continually evolving way, it's about how my relationship with my dad continues to be the impetus for my own ever-deepening and richer understanding of the meaning of God and Love for me and what it means to live not only from but also as God, as Love—as *me*.

Section 1

The Excavation Begins
(Stories)

Chapter 1

A Foundation of Fear

"When we tell stories about the family without judgment and without instant analysis, the literal persons turn into characters in a drama and isolated episodes reveal themselves as themes in a great saga. Family history is transformed into myth."

— Thomas Moore, *Care of the Soul*

When my dad died, my sister, Larissa, and I declared we would be the ones to give the eulogy. Although there were many other people who knew him better and had spent more time with him—especially in recent years—we both agreed that if we left the eulogy to his friends or colleagues, we would most likely end up hearing about his list of accomplishments. We'd end up hearing more about the jobs he'd had and the work he'd done over his decades-long career as a world-travelling management consultant—something more akin to a résumé or CV rather than who he was as a man. The thing was, though, both of us had had tenuous relationships with him our entire lives, and when it came down to what I was going to say, I grappled with how to talk about him honestly while still honouring the pain, confusion, and anger I was feeling. Even though I was in my late forties when he died, I could still hear my dad's voice in my head:

- "You're not good enough."
- "You're not smart enough."
- "You don't have what it takes."

I was also very aware that my ten-year-old daughter and my slightly older niece and nephew would be present. Even though I didn't plan on making my dad out to be a saint, I also didn't want them, or anyone else present, to hear how hard, painful, and confusing it had been to grow up with him as my dad.

I was also very aware that my mom would be there. She'd been my dad's first wife, and he, the love of her life. Although they had divorced after fifteen years of marriage, and she had been the one to leave, I knew my dad still held a very special place in her heart.

After days of wondering what I was going to say, I furiously scribbled and crossed out thoughts, notes, and anecdotes in the car on the way to the funeral. Trying to ignore a lifetime's sting of those three phrases that seemed so firmly etched in my brain and on my soul, I finally decided I would just let it go, suck it up, and trust that once I got up to the podium, whatever wanted to be said would end up being shared with as much diplomacy and grace as was mine to muster.

As my sister and I walked up to the podium together, with me still wondering what would come out of my mouth, I stepped up, took a deep breath, and said:

"Growing up my father's daughter was not easy…"

* * *

My parents both grew up in Edmonton after their families emigrated from Ukraine. My mom, an only child, came over with her mom just after the Second World War. Shortly after they arrived in Canada, my grandmother met and married my grandfather. He adopted my mom, and she grew up in a loving home, surrounded by family, where both parents, extended family, and the community were devoted to her.

My dad came over with his parents just before the end of the war. Ten years later, his younger sister was born. The home they grew up in was very different.

My parents' first date was more the result of a negotiation between my grandparents than it was two teenagers going out for a much-anticipated date. My dad had already asked another girl to a dance. He was told by his dad, however, that if he wanted to borrow the car that night, he'd have to take my mom. My mom, who was two years younger and found my dad handsome but arrogant, didn't really want to go. But go she did because her father had told her to. According to my mom, the mediocre evening ended when my dad tried to get fresh, at which point she demanded he take her home.

Two years later, however, they reconnected, sparks flew, and they fell head over heels in love. They married young, with my mom already three months pregnant with me.

After fifteen years, two kids, three cats, and a lifetime of volatility, they got divorced.

Although life was less than perfect within our family, and my memories of growing up are fragmented, I do remember seeing my parents happy. I remember them laughing, singing, celebrating, and dancing together. When they danced, even friends and members of the community would comment on how perfectly matched they were, right down to their height. So when my mom announced she was leaving my dad, my sister and I, our family, and the community were shocked.

* * *

When I was little, I thought my dad was the smartest, most handsome and most charming man alive. He was funny, a great storyteller, an excellent conversationalist, and a gourmet cook. He had a rich bass voice and sang beautifully. He was a great dancer and could be the life of the party. When I was little, I wanted to be just like him.

For most of my life I was told I looked, sounded, and acted just like my dad. I was smart, talented, and charismatic, just like he was. I also happened to laugh like him, speak with the same cadence, and he and I shared a lot of the same mannerisms. When I was younger, it felt amazing to be told I was so much like the person I idolized.

As I grew older, however, it also began to feel like a burden, even a curse. Because along with the smarts, talent, and charisma, there was confusion, judgement, anger, and fear—lots and lots of anger and an ever-evolving amount of fear.

Along with his charm, my dad had a volatile temper. He could also be physically, emotionally, and psychologically abusive. By my teens, I wasn't sure my dad loved or even liked me. By the time I was a young adult, I wasn't sure I liked or loved him.

One of my earliest memories is of my mom holding me as we both listened to my younger sister screaming and crying while our dad beat her with a belt. I don't remember what she'd done to make him so angry. What I do remember—because this punishment was par for the course—was feeling terrifed because I knew I was next. I sat quietly in my mom's arms (what she was feeling at the time, I can only imagine), waiting for my turn to come. I was around three and my sister, one.

I don't remember how many times this happened. Because toddlers generally didn't hang around talking about how their parents disciplined them, to me, this was normal.

Another memory from around the same time is of me standing in front of the tall, narrow glass window in our entranceway. As the sun poured through the rippled pane, I became fascinated by the long, winding S-like crack in the glass. I remember taking my tiny index finger, and with pure, childlike curiosity, slowly tracing the S as I ran my finger along the curve of the crack with the sunlight glimmering and shimmering through the glass.

Suddenly, my dad was beside me, screaming at me, asking me how I could be so stupid and careless. He wrenched my tiny hand away from the glass, still yelling, as I realized I'd cut my tiny finger and was bleeding—something I hadn't even noticed because I'd been so entranced by the S in the window and the sunlight dancing through the glass. Although likely meant as a protective reflex, my dad's anger turned childlike innocence, curiosity, and wonder into fear and shame in a split second. There was no in between.

As I grew up, what triggered my dad's anger could also range from something of great significance (say, crashing the car) to something seemingly less so (like not finishing a piece of blood sausage on my dinner plate). It felt like there was no way to know when he might erupt or how intense the explosion might be. It was almost impossible to know what his priorities were—like the time I was eight or nine and a rock the size of my fist flew out from under the lawn mower as I was cutting the grass. It hit me in the shin, causing my leg to bruise, welt, and bleed immediately. When I went inside, crying and asking for help, my dad insisted I finish mowing the lawn first, thinking that would somehow teach me a lesson to be more careful next time.

As my sister and I got older, the physical beatings dissipated, but the explosive anger, unattainable expectations, and shaming that occurred when those expectations weren't met grew in intensity. I can still remember one physical altercation in my teens after my mom and dad had separated and we were spending the weekend with my dad.

While my dad I were screaming at each other with my sister in her room, I accidentally knocked off my dad's glasses. Fuelled by his rage, he lunged at me, threw me onto the ground, and started choking me. I remember thinking if it hadn't been for my younger sister intervening, I felt sure he was going to kill me.

Again, I don't remember what I'd done that had made him so angry. As the altercation escalated, however, there was a point where I remember thinking, *I've just knocked off Tato's (dad in Ukrainian) glasses, something mama told me never to do. It means he can't see, which means he has no control. Having no control is making him angrier. He's already screaming and yelling at me. I'm trapped and don't know what to do. Now he's lunging at me. He's so strong, I can't fight him off. Oh, my God, I'm on the ground and he's choking me. I think he's going to kill me!*

It all happened in a split second, as if time had slowed down and expanded exponentially. It was as if a blind rage had taken control of him, and if not for my sister jumping on his back and screaming for him to stop, he may not have realized what he was doing until it was too late.

What I also remember is that immediately afterward, my dad drove my sister and a close friend to an overnight scouting camp. I was no longer allowed to go because of whatever I'd done, and he let me know in no uncertain terms that he'd deal with me when he got back. The feeling of dread and terror was enough to drive me to start packing, thinking the only thing I could do was run away.

As I threw things into my bag, it slowly started to sink in that I had no money. I had nowhere to go and no one I could talk to about this—not even my mom. She'd recently left my dad and I was still so angry with her for breaking up our family. No one would believe me, except for my sister, because she was the only one who'd been there and had seen what had happened. As I began to unpack and put my things away, I also prepared myself for the worst.

Then the unexpected happened. My dad got back and told me to get in the car. For sixty minutes, in complete, stone-cold silence, we drove to the overnight camp. When we arrived, he told me to get the hell out of the car. As I stepped out of the car, I was greeted by the camp counsellor and my cheerful, enthusiastic friends, wondering why I was so late. As I closed the car door, my dad left without saying a word.

I ended up lying to my friends, making up a story about my dad finding cocaine in one of my stereo speakers and completely flipping out because of that. Whatever the real reason had been, it had felt so tame in comparison to my made-up cover story. I honestly thought there was no way my friends would believe that my dad had gotten as angry and violent as he had because of whatever actually happened. Being on the receiving end of that kind of explosive anger repeatedly over the course of years and decades—anger that was often paired with inconsistent behaviour—can and did take a very profound toll.

As a result, for most of my life, I lived in fear, and not just of my dad. I was constantly afraid of accidentally or inadvertently saying or doing something that would give my dad or anyone—especially any authority figure—reason to get angry. So for most of my childhood, I tried so hard to please the adults in my life—my parents, my teachers; especially my dad—by being as close to perfect as possible.

I excelled in school, music, dance, Ukrainian scouting, and Ukrainian school. I brought home A's and A-plusses, came in first place, and won gold medals. I also tried to be on my best behaviour in social situations that involved my dad, trying to avoid anything that might embarrass him in any way.

Perfection meant accolades. Perfection meant smiles, hugs, and kudos from my dad. Perfection meant safety and peace. Perfection was my protection.

For most of my childhood and early teens, on the outside, I was a rock star! On the inside, though—especially into my teenage years—I felt more and more like a taped and patched-up Humpty Dumpty who'd fallen off the wall too many times to tell. Being perfect all the time was hard work. It felt like I was constantly holding my breath while teetering on the brink of "the wall," wondering whether my grades and my behaviour or I were good enough to keep my dad's anger at bay. I wondered whether any of it was enough to keep me from falling and shattering into a million pieces below for good.

* * *

I was fifteen when my parents split up. I remember being surprised, wondering why and whether they would end up getting back together (something that would come up again and again for me, even into adulthood). What I remember more prominently was being given the choice as to which parent my sister and I wanted to live with.

A judge had deemed my sister and me old enough to make that decision for ourselves, so we did. Even though I still felt terrified of my dad, he was the one staying in our family home, with the car and my piano. Staying with him would mean some semblance of normalcy, or at least the familiar. Going with my mom would mean starting something new. I was also vehemently angry with my mom because it had been her decision to leave.

By that point, my dad was also travelling for work regularly and was only home a few days a month—a teenager's dream! So how awful could it be? I also knew my sister would go with our mom. So even though there was a certain amount of trepidation in staying with our dad, and I had considered going with our mom, I decided to stay. After all, there would also be the perks of being alone, with a car, in an empty house, and with a credit card to "shop for groceries."

It would be about twenty years later, during a heated argument the day after my dad's second wedding that my sister and I would discover why we had each chosen the parent we'd chosen, even though we had both considered going with the other. *Neither of us wanted to leave either parent alone.*

Knowing how sad, confused, and angry *we* each felt as our family home was breaking up, we both felt obligated to somehow take care of our parents. So, my sister went to live with our mom, and I ended up staying with our dad.

* * *

After my parents separated, my life started to visibly fall apart. I couldn't understand what was happening. I felt like a complete failure and like things were only getting worse. It was getting harder and harder to get through each day without falling apart. It was getting harder and harder to keep it together.

After a string of failures—school grades plummeting, being forced by my parents to give up ballet, loss of interest in music, becoming disillusioned with Ukrainian scouts, and not caring anymore about Ukrainian school—I decided perhaps it'd be better to not be around at all. If I weren't around at all, I wouldn't have to deal with all the pain, anger, and fear that had been my foundation for living for so long. If I weren't around at all, I wouldn't cause my dad to be so angry. I decided it'd be better to just die. So I attempted suicide.

What ended up being a carefully planned event, with my dad out of town, and no reason for my mom or anyone else to stop by that evening, turned into a night in the emergency room. I vaguely remember muttering something to my mom (who'd stopped by unannounced) about the flavours of maxi pads while high as a kite on pills and booze. And after having my stomach pumped— so I could feel better, not because my life was in any great danger (the cocktail of pills and booze I'd consumed wouldn't have been strong enough to kill me)—I ended up in hospital under observation for a few days.

When my friends came to visit me in the hospital, I remember feeling so embarrassed and ashamed. I couldn't even succeed at suicide. This was just another failure to add to the already growing list of disappointments.

It, however, was one of the few times I'd felt seen by my dad. He came home from a business trip early to see *me*. Then he stayed home for a while, cancelling some of his business trips to make sure I went back to school and so he could keep in touch with the teachers to see how things were going. It's one of the rare times during my youth where I remember thinking my dad actually cared about me, like a normal dad would—like a dad was *supposed to*. He hadn't come back because of my grades or some award I might've won (which I wasn't winning anymore anyway). He came back for *me*, for his daughter.

That entire suicide debacle prompted my parents to send me to a child psychologist. After only a few visits, I told the therapist what he wanted to hear. I assured him that I hadn't really wanted to die, that I was only trying to get attention, and that I would never try anything like that again. I guess I was convincing enough because he then assured my parents that I was no longer a threat to myself and could be trusted again to be left alone.

So my dad went back to his business trips. And I continued along my path of self-destruction under the guise of "being cool" and aloof, with just enough presence and participation in life so that my mom and the school wouldn't be concerned and call him. At least that's what it seemed like at the time.

I barely graduated high school and dropped out of university after only three months. By this time, I had my own apartment, a job, a radio show at the campus university station, and some friends I'd made through the radio station (at the university I'd dropped out of). I was slowly beginning to feel like I was finding my way.

As I settled into this new phase, life turned into one party after another as I bounced from one party to the next, one live music gig to the next. Drugs, alcohol, and blackouts became part and parcel of the new, independent, fun life I was living. In between the parties, the gigs, the drugs, and booze, though—in the light of day—I would feel confused, like I didn't quite fit in, like I was an imposter. No matter how much I partied or drank, it was never enough to feel good about myself for long. Feeling like a fraud never completely went away.

* * *

Just after I turned eighteen, my dad told me he was selling our family home and asked if I wanted to move to Toronto with him. I jumped at the chance. Just like switching high schools a year earlier, moving to another city meant leaving behind all the pain, drama, fear, and disappointment. It was the beginning of something new and exciting, something different. And even though I was still afraid of him, now that I was a young adult, my dad and I found common ground in drinking, music, and gourmet food. Essentially, as long as I "partied" with him, things were okay. If it went any deeper than that, though, the pain that came with the anger and fear from long before would once again rear its ugly head.

We lived together for a year. My dad was out of town for work most of the time. When he was home, we didn't spend much time together. But we did spend time with my aunt Vera—my dad's younger, much cooler, and extraordinarily compassionate sister—who'd become like a second mom to me after we moved to Toronto.

There were ten years between my dad and my aunt. My dad had left their family home at eighteen when she was only eight. As such, they hadn't grown up together. Now, as adults, it was like they knew of each other, but didn't really know one another.

My aunt adored her older brother, but she also had her challenges with him. A gifted, accomplished, and well-respected doctor, she was also a super smart, beautiful, charismatic woman with an amazing community of friends and loved ones. Yet, my dad would still often treat her as that bratty little sister he'd left behind at eighteen, coming across as the know-it-all older brother.

I remember one Ukrainian Christmas Eve when the three of us cooked our traditional twelve-course meal.

Imagine bright fuchsia borscht, heady with the aroma of beet kvas, garlic, and wild mushrooms simmering on the stove. The scent of freshly chopped dill on the cutting board for sprinkling over the borscht and gefilte fish wafting through the kitchen. Wild Atlantic salmon prepped with lemon and salt, lying in wait, ready to be baked. Big pots of water boiling furiously, awaiting the ushka (tiny "pig's ears" dumplings stuffed with wild mushrooms and garlic—a favourite dish served only at Christmastime) and a variety of varennyky (aka perogies). There were the savoury potato and onion, sauerkraut, the more indulgent prune and cinnamon, and poppyseed.

Then there were the ingredients for the kutia—the most traditional and symbolic dish of the meal—waiting to be mixed with the greatest of care. Boiled wheat, poppyseeds, and honey—another favourite, served only at Christmastime. The wheat symbolizes the work and blessings of the land and the eternal cycle of life. The poppyseeds symbolize wealth, riches, and fertility. The honey represents good health and the sweetness of life that brings everything together. It is the dish that begins the sacred meal, with each person present receiving a blessing along with a spoonful of this reverential dish. Traditionally, after the initial blessing, the head of the household takes a spoonful of kutia and tosses it to the ceiling. Depending on how and what sticks, one can foretell what the coming year will be like.

At one point during this particular Christmas Eve, Vera and my dad argued, and my aunt left the kitchen in tears. "Les, I think I made your aunt cry," my dad said, a slight smirk on his face. Even though I don't think he meant it maliciously, he didn't realize the sting of his words, tone, and actions (which were akin to bullying) on his sister mere moments before.

The following year, after returning from a summer job in Edmonton, I moved out of my dad's place and into a shared house with three roommates. I continued drinking to excess, using recreational drugs, ventured into promiscuity, struggled with trying to fit in, and ultimately spiralled into another depression. I lied, cheated, stole, and came up with a zillion excuses to remain firmly grounded in seething anger. Even though I wasn't fully aware of why I felt so angry, this anger continued to fuel my self-destructive behaviour.

I had friends. I worked. I appeared fully functional. I could even be the life of the party. But as much as I tried to fit in and please everyone around me, I felt less and less comfortable in my own skin. I knew I was smart and capable, but I was also afraid and felt small. Life just felt so hard so much of the time. And even though I'd just entered my twenties, I felt so incredibly exhausted.

One day, a couple of years later, I woke up, seriously contemplating suicide again. I spent a few days cleaning up and giving away my things at the office and began to formulate a plan. Bizarrely enough, as I went around the office, giving away trinkets I'd amassed over the years I'd worked there, my friend Glenn—who years later would become my husband—actually asked me, "You're not planning on topping yourself, are you?"

A few days later, I stood at the top of the Don Valley Bridge for a long time—my James Stewart from *It's a Wonderful Life* moment—wondering whether anyone would miss me if I jumped and ended it all. Instead of jumping, though, something inside me pulled me away from the edge and directed me toward the subway station nearby.

I soon found myself en route to Mississauga (a neighbouring city I barely knew how to navigate) via subway, then bus, to seek out my aunt. I eventually arrived at her clinic, only to find that she was home sick with a debilitating migraine that day. The receptionist offered to call her at home, but I thanked her and said no, thinking, *I've made it this far, I might as well keep going*, eventually making my way over to her place via local transit.

I'm pretty sure she was just as surprised to see me as I was to be standing at her door. I don't remember what happened next, but I do know we spent the day together and clearly, I didn't jump off any bridge. A few days, weeks, or maybe months later, I eventually called her and told her I couldn't live like this anymore. I couldn't understand what was happening to me and that I needed help.

Over the next several years, with the support of my aunt, I met and worked with a handful of psychologists and therapists to address my depression and addiction to alcohol. It hadn't even occurred to me that I might have a problem with alcohol or drugs until the first psychiatrist I met with said he wouldn't agree to treat me until I dealt with my alcoholism. I didn't like him anyway and had no intention of working with him, so it was no big deal. It also felt more than a bit insulting to be told I abused alcohol and that until I stopped drinking, there was no way he could work with me.

I was so angry. What could he possibly know about me and how could he possibly call *me* an alcoholic?!

However, the concept of feeling utterly broken became more and more apparent as I found myself spiralling downward into a pit of despair.

It felt as though that wrongness or brokenness could rub off on and infect someone I'd come to like or even love. So, I'd withdraw from life time and time again in an effort to "save" those around me from the anguish I was experiencing. This ominous feeling could last for days, even weeks—a massive mental and emotional block that kept me from moving forward in life in any kind of healthy, proactive, or life-affirming way. It's what would keep me from having any kind of truly intimate or trusting relationship with anyone for decades, even though deep down inside, that's not only what I craved, but what I needed.

Thankfully, with my aunt's help, I eventually found a therapist I liked and felt safe enough to work with on and off throughout my adult life until she retired and I "graduated." I know it was largely due to the compassion, attentiveness, and support I experienced during my sessions with her that I was able to rediscover the power, confidence, and resilience that had been buried and hidden under so much pain, anger, and fear for so long.

When it came to the alcohol, it took a while, but eventually, begrudgingly, I quit drinking. Once I quit drinking, I stopped using drugs. As I let go of the booze and drugs, the booze and drugs left my system. However, all the pain, anger, and fear—the trauma of my younger days—came alive in new, more vivid ways. Pain, anger, and fear wove their way into every relationship, every decision, every job, *every part of my life*. These feelings shaped how I showed up as a spouse, friend, parent, employer, daughter, sister—even as I dove into my spiritual/consciousness studies a few decades later.

The traumatic residue, the very foundation and underpinning of my life, would continue to be the lens through which I viewed the world and myself for years to come. I'd constantly doubt and second-guess my decisions. I was convinced I wouldn't amount to anything of significance because I wasn't smart, educated, or talented enough to do anything of any substance.

I saw friends move forward in their education, into higher paying jobs, building careers, having relationships, buying houses and condos and cars, and going on vacations, while I continued to barely make ends meet. For so many years, I felt left behind. Even though there were things about life I could appreciate and even enjoy, it felt like there was this underlying, nagging disappointment that I hadn't "made it" in life yet. I should've been making more money. I should've had a house already. I should've been in a committed relationship. I should be more of a grown-up, living a grown-up life by now. Yet all I continued to feel was, *I have no idea who I am or what I want to do with my life.*

* * *

On the day of the traditional gift opening the day after my sister's first wedding (which also happened to be my birthday), something within me shifted. To celebrate my birthday and as a thank you for being her maid of honour, my sister and her new husband gave me a Braun stand-up mixer. When I initially saw the box, I thought to myself, *There's no way that's what's really in there. They must've just used the box for something else.*

However, when I saw the brand-spankin'-new mixer inside— just like the one our baba (grandmother) had used—I felt an immediate rush of inspiration. I realized that perhaps *this* was what I was meant to do in life. I had already received a beautiful book on bread making from a friend, along with another food-themed gift from another friend. I had always loved cooking and baking and marvelled at how talented my baba, my great aunt (my baba's sister), and several of my mom's cousins were.

I remember thinking, *Everyone's gotta eat.* Not only that, but food could also make people feel so happy. Thanks to the amazing cooks and bakers in my family, I also knew there was so much creativity to be expressed through food, whether it be savoury or sweet. And because there was no end to creativity with food, there would always be something new to learn.

For my entire life, my love of cooking and baking had been something I'd taken for granted. It had never occurred to me that it could be something I'd want to do as a career. Now, thanks to these three marvelous gifts, for the first time in my adult life, I felt like I actually *knew* what I wanted to do. And it felt amazing!

The three gifts I received for my birthday inspired me to take a vegetarian-cooking course. This course led me to a job at one of Toronto's most prominent bakeries and gourmet food stores. During my time at this bakery, I discovered my love of working with chocolate, which led me to take some courses in chocolate making and cake decorating, which in turn led me to a couple of incredible jobs as a restaurant pastry chef. Eventually, I started my own business, which led to the founding of Toronto's first organic, sustainably minded pastry and chocolate shop—LPK's Culinary Groove.

I had also met and fallen in love with Glenn, who'd not only captured but cracked open my heart and soul in ways I didn't even know were possible. I had friends, a community, a life partner, and a new career/business I was building. In the midst of all of this growth, Glenn and I got married and bought a house. My life was starting to feel good, and I was actually beginning to feel good about myself.

By this time, my dad had moved overseas, and I had very little contact with him. He'd married and divorced a second time and eventually moved to and settled in Ukraine, where he ultimately met and married his third wife.

Over the next decade or so, as I continued to build my life in Toronto, my dad rooted himself in his homeland. I'd hear about his endeavours from my aunt, my sister, even my mom, but I didn't go to any great lengths to keep in contact with him. He would send me the funniest anecdotes and stories by email (some of which I shared in his eulogy), but other than that, "out of sight, out of mind" worked well, and for the time being, it felt fine.

Even with all of that goodness, though, even as I got my own life together, I still had my own challenges with anger. Over time, I realized how much like my dad I'd become. When things didn't go my way, I would erupt. I would throw things, slam phones against the wall, I would scream at people, I would lash out at the drop of a hat.

Sometimes I'd even let people know I wasn't yelling at them as much as I was letting off steam about what they'd done or something that had happened. I'd rationalize it all because I wasn't physically hurting anyone. I was just expressing my anger in what I considered to be relatively normal, healthy ways. After all, I'd heard time and time again, if you don't express your anger, it'll continue to fester, and will eventually explode no matter what.

So now, not only did I look and talk like my dad, but I also erupted and exploded with anger—just like my dad. The intensity of that anger could sometimes feel so all-consuming, I would scare even myself. Afterward, I would feel such profound shame at having treated my husband, employees, family, or friends so horribly. It felt awful—beyond embarrassing, beyond mortifying. I'd feel less than small, less than insignificant. I wanted to just run away and hide.

There were many, many times over my adult life when severe or disproportionate anger would suddenly rear its insidious head. However, nowhere was it more prevalent than during the course of opening, running, and eventually closing my "dream-come-true-turned-nightmare" organic, sustainably minded bakery, LPK's Culinary Groove. More on that later.

* * *

One day, after not hearing from my dad for some time, I got word from my aunt that my dad was sick. He'd been diagnosed with Stage 4 colorectal cancer. There was no Stage 5. My aunt insisted he leave Ukraine and come back to Canada—Toronto specifically—for treatment. And just like that, after over a decade, my dad was back in my life again.

By then, I'd been on my healing journey for a bit and was more curious about what my dad was going through and how others were behaving, rather than feeling anything specific about his having been diagnosed with cancer. I was also incredibly busy with work and felt my business and my family were what required my utmost attention.

What I was very aware of, however, was that my dad had never met my daughter, who was already seven. I suspected Mylana could probably have a totally different relationship with him than I'd had and didn't want to stand in the way of whatever that relationship could be. My dad was back in my life again, and it looked like my daughter would finally have her grandfather in hers.

Watching Mylana and my dad develop a beautiful, loving, fun relationship—where he came in with some trepidation, and she with none—was amazing. They would play and joke around together. He delighted in bringing her beautiful children's books from Ukraine. They would also just sit and talk. Eventually, she even went over for a couple of sleepovers.

I still recall—a couple of days before their first sleepover—my dad calling to tell me he'd gone out and bought organic, vegetarian, gluten-free food so Mylana would have plenty to eat when she stayed over. I was grateful, but also dumbfounded and confused.

The man Mylana was getting to know was not the man I grew up with, and I had a hard time reconciling that. Over the years, my dad had softened. He'd relaxed. He smiled more. He was still just as opinionated, but he was different. I realized that I wasn't seeing *my dad* as much as I was seeing *Mylana's grandfather*. As I watched this relationship blossom, I could see and feel how much they both loved and delighted in each other and what a gift they were to each other.

For me, though, as his daughter, as much as I loved that Mylana now had her grandfather in her life, I also found myself feeling heartbroken and sad. I'd missed out on having the loving, caring dad who was now showing up as a loving, attentive grandfather.

One day, my aunt came to me and said, "I know there's stuff between you and your dad. I know there's a painful legacy there. But he's going to die, and you have to step up. Please spend some time with him. He loves you and he needs you even though he won't tell you."

At the time, and throughout his treatment, I remember thinking, *How can you know he's going to die? How can you possibly know anything, just because you're a doctor? Maybe he will, maybe he won't. Just because the statistics aren't in favour of him living more than two and a half years after his diagnosis, why is it a done deal for you?*

Not only was there confusion about who this man was now vs. the man I grew up with, but I was also angry at my aunt and others who'd already decided he had one foot in the grave. I felt even angrier because I was being asked to spend time with him when I had so many other things in my life I wanted to focus on. The exhaustion I'd been feeling for decades was now beginning to feel suffocating.

The next eighteen months were hard—not just challenging—*hard*. Every Sunday, after I'd worked back-to-back farmers' markets on Saturday and Sunday, with a night of prep in between (which meant little or no sleep), we'd have family dinner at my house. My aunt would bring my dad and a couple of hours later, they'd head home. It felt nearly impossible to work through my exhaustion and sleep deprivation, and I was so grateful for Glenn and his ability to entertain my dad as I made dinner. I was also super thankful that my aunt and Mylana were there because it meant I could just focus on dinner and not really have to participate.

I was also grateful that my sister, Larissa, flew in from Victoria a few times to visit. When she did, she stayed with our dad. As a nurse, she was used to attending to people who required care. It was also amazing because not only did she and my dad get along much better than he and I did, but it also meant I could pull away and still not have to actively participate in cultivating any kind of relationship with him.

Then one day, when he and my sister arrived for dinner, I saw him slowly hobble up the stairs to our living room, enduring the immense pain of not having any padding left on the bottoms of his feet (a side effect of chemo). As I watched him put on a brave face, I knew that would be the last time he'd ever set foot in our home. In that moment, I could *feel* my dad was going to die soon and such profound sadness and grief overcame my entire being.

* * *

I felt I'd wasted time. I felt I'd been selfish. I didn't know my dad any better than I did before he'd returned to Toronto, and now, he was literally breaking down and wasting away in front of my eyes.

My aunt and I, a few close friends of his, and eventually some home care nurses, ended up taking turns being with him until his wife arrived from Ukraine. The last pleasant memory I have of my dad is how he thoroughly enjoyed and polished off a simple, nourishing meal of salmon and sautéed vegetables—the last meal I prepared for him. He ate it with such gusto, picking at everything slowly and deliberately with a toothpick because he'd become too weak to manoeuvre a fork. I don't remember what we talked about or if we talked much at all, just that he really enjoyed that meal and that I'd made it for him. He was happy. I was happy. For a brief time that evening, we were actually happy *together*.

A couple of weeks later, with my dad's health deteriorating, his wife arrived from Ukraine with her immigration papers in hand. She was shocked when she saw him, as she hadn't spoken to him in several weeks and when she had, she'd only seen him from the neck up. Regardless, her attitude was inspirational to me because even though she really wanted him to live, she said it wasn't about what she wanted, but how she could help him be comfortable—how she could be of service.

That's when I realized that's what I needed to do, too. No matter what had happened in the past, no matter how I felt about my dad, this was where we were *now*. I could choose to see him through the eyes of love—no matter how foreign it felt—or I could choose to focus on the pain, anger, and fear of the past. I decided it was time to let go of the past and see my dad for who he truly was, rather than who I remembered him to be.

During those last few weeks is when he kept repeating the phrase "God is Love." Even though I didn't understand or appreciate their meaning at the time, I repeated those words back to him.

A few weeks after his wife arrived from Ukraine, my dad died in his sleep.

I remember my dad telling me that when my grandfather died, it took my dad five years to get over his father's death. At the time, I thought it strange because I remembered they'd had a very strained relationship. There was much about his dad he admired, but there was also a lot of pain, anger, and fear at the root of their relationship. I found it kind of bizarre it could take someone so long to get over a parent's death when they hadn't really gotten along in the first place.

Now, here I was, navigating the aftermath of my dad's death. The days, weeks, and months following my dad's death were some of the most challenging times for me. I had trouble understanding why I felt so sad—why I'd be feeling fine one moment, only to completely break down the next. I also felt increasingly bewildered as I met my dad's friends from the Ukrainian community or the church choir he sang with. They would all comment on how much I looked and sounded like him. They would talk about what an amazing, generous, kind, and compassionate man he was—a prince among men. They would tell me how lucky I was to have had a father like him.

It was like living in a parallel universe. I could see their mouths moving, even hear what they were saying, but I had such trouble understanding how they could possibly be talking about the man I'd known as my dad. It wasn't until a few years later, as I became more immersed in my spiritual/consciousness studies that I would discover and really begin to understand what an integral part of my beingness my dad had been and continues to be. How curious it would be to discover that it would take me about five years to get over *my* dad's death, too.

Today, seven years after my dad's death, much of the anger has dissipated, but the grief for a father-daughter relationship I desired but never experienced can still take me by surprise— including while writing this book. With that grief can also come the doubts, the second-guessing, and the fear. And today, even though I now consciously choose to focus my attention on the Infinite Creativity, Resilience, and Love I know myself *and* my dad to be, there are still those occasions when that fear (which can still sound like my dad's voice, but is really my own) resurfaces, trying to convince me:

- "You're not good enough."
- "You're not smart enough."
- "You don't have what it takes."

Today, when those words come up, I know they are just that— *words.* I also know that even though they may have originally come from my dad, those words are not his. I know I'm not the only one to have experienced the trauma of a lifetime of pain, anger, and fear. I'm not the only one to have heard those or similar words repeatedly, feeling their residual sting in every fibre of my being for years. I know these words are not who I am. I also know they are not my dad.

I have come to understand they are words of generations passed— family, community, culture, and the global collective—forever floating in the infinite sea of memory, history, and possibility. I also now understand that I am always *choosing* what I identify with by where I put my attention and energy. I get to decide— do I want to continually retell and relive the pain, anger, and fear of the past or do I want to focus on the Infinite Creativity, Resilience, and Love that I know myself—and my dad—to be? I get to choose, and I choose Love.

Growing up my father's daughter was not easy. However, I am so grateful to have had the dad I had. I am so eternally grateful for our volatile relationship—for the decades of pain, anger, and fear. I am so grateful he parented in the best way he knew how, no matter how hard it was for me or how challenging it may have been for him. I'm also so, so, so very grateful to have been present during those last few weeks of his life as he comforted himself by repeating, "God is Love."

When I think back to the phrase "God is Love," I think of my dad coming to terms with his own mortality, of wrestling with the life he'd lived vs. the life he'd perhaps desired and was capable of living. I think of him ultimately acquiescing—even though there was a part of him that *really* wanted to live—to whatever experience was his to have after his physical body was done. I also think of him realizing that no matter what pain, anger, and fear he may have lived through, when all is said and done, all is God, God is Love, and Love is all there is.

Chapter 2

A Story of Failure

"It is in the nature of things to be drawn to the very experiences that will spoil our innocence, transform our lives, and give us necessary complexity and depth."

— Thomas Moore, *Care of the Soul*

I still remember the feeling of anticipation mixed with dread, layered with defeat, bound up in resignation, as I sat at my computer, waiting to hit the *enter* button. The decision had been made. The email had been written. And as soon as I hit the *enter* button on my laptop, everyone would know…*Everyone* would know what an epic failure my bakery had been.

I took a breath, and knowing there was no going back, hit *enter*. It was done.

I got up from my desk, walked slowly through the basement and up the stairs. I walked through the kitchen and past my staff. As I entered the retail portion of my bakery, one of our regular customers walked in, phone in hand, staring at it, then us, in disbelief. It felt so dramatic, so pivotal, so heartbreaking all at the same time. It was a total movie moment.

"Is this true…?" he asked.

I'd just sent out an email to everyone I knew stating that, after only four years in business, it was with much sadness, anger, and disappointment, that we were closing down my beloved organic, sustainable, gluten-free, primarily vegan bakery. As I looked at our customer, still staring at us in disbelief, all I could do was nod, turn around, walk back into the kitchen, and burst into tears.

My heart ached. Even though the decision had been made a few months beforehand and my loyal and committed staff had kept the news to themselves—not even sharing it with those nearest and dearest to them—now that the news was public, it made the whole ordeal seem even more surreal, even more devastating.

As the news spread, the emails of disbelief, empathy, and compassion started to pour in. And so did the questions. Articles were written in newspapers and magazines, and everyone wanted to know what happened.

"But you were doing so well… "

"We had no idea… "

"I'm so sorry to hear… "

Eventually, as it dawned on our customers that we were closing for good, people also began to ask, "Where will we get our organic, vegan, gluten-free Nanaimo Bars?" and "Where will we be able to find our Spicy Chèvre Noir Shortbread Cookies?"

Over the next two and a half months, with the help, support, and love of my staff, friends, family, and the community that had built up around us, I began the painstaking process of dismantling and letting go of what had truly been my dream—a high-end pastry and chocolate shop committed to using certified organic and fair-trade ingredients while championing local organic farmers and food artisans. Not only that, but we had also offered high-end quality baked goods and desserts that catered to those with various dietary requirements (regardless of the reason). My bakery had been a testament to successfully creating beautiful, delicious desserts and baked goods that happened to be gluten-free and plant-based, respecting the environment in the process.

My work and business had been the number one priority in my life for nearly two decades—coming before my family, my marriage, my friends, and me—and the seemingly epic failure of my bakery was beyond soul-crushing.

As my skeleton staff and I mustered to fulfill every last order, to honour as many financial commitments as possible, and to continue embodying our mission of "Delighting our clients by treating them, our ingredients, and our world with love and respect," all I kept hearing was my dad's voice over and over and over again in my head. "You'll never succeed as an entrepreneur. *You don't have what it takes.*"

* * *

When I was little, I loved watching my baba bake. She, along with her older sister and three of my mom's cousins, were extraordinarily talented home bakers and cooks. Whether it be a wedding, funeral, birthday, christening, Sunday brunch, or weekend marathon of card playing, it seemed there was always something worth celebrating. Where there was celebration, there was food!

I remember elaborate buffet tables filled with platters of tiny appetizers, including stuffed puff pastry, mini quiches, charcuterie and cheese plates, pickled beets and horseradish, and pickles. I remember roasted duck, goose, and ham accompanied by mushroom gravy infused with fresh dill from the garden, with potatoes, carrots, homemade spätzle or homemade varennyky (perogies) alongside refreshing cucumber and other salads. But most of all, I remember the desserts—beautifully crafted multilayered hazelnut and almond tortes with mocha buttercream and my baba's carrot cake (made with carrots from her garden) with a classic cream cheese frosting. There could also be napoleons, plum cake, apricot cake, and deep-fried khrusty (crispy, flaky, deep-fried dough twists) lightly dusted with icing sugar.

And then there were the doughnuts. *Mmm, doughnuts...* (Sorry, Homer Simpson moment). The fresh, homemade, brioche-style doughnuts were a beautiful sun-kissed bronze on the outside and golden yellow on the inside, and were moist, light, and bready like a cloud. My baba would make them plain. My aunt Lialia would fill them with her homemade rose jam. And my aunt Sonia would fill them with plum preserves. My baba actually had a stand-up freezer in her bedroom filled with ready-made tortes, cakes, pastries, and cookies, all carefully wrapped in plastic wrap (with toothpicks inserted in the iced cakes so as not to mar the finish) and then wrapped in another protective layer of tin foil, just in case someone should happen to stop by for tea.

A passion for food, especially baking, was in my blood.

When I first started working with food for a living, it was an extension of what I had grown up with, of what I already knew. It was about the basics. But then—especially after I got into chocolate making—I realized the artistry and creativity that came out of working with sugar, butter, flour, and chocolate. I began to realize what was possible and how working with food as a medium sparked my imagination. It was no longer about just following recipes, it was more like, *What do these ingredients want to become?*

How amazing, I thought, that for some people, mixing water and flour would make a paste akin to glue (papier mâché anyone?), yet for others—especially those for whom the science and chemistry of baking was just as important as the way food tasted—mixing water with flour could be the start of a delicious sauce, or a pancake, or a sponge for bread, and so on and so forth. By adding in some sugar, eggs, chocolate, fruit, and more, there was no limit to what could be created with food.

More importantly, what I also came to realize was that great food wasn't an "either-or" situation. You could have great-tasting food that also looked exquisite and enticing. Later on in my career, I'd push the boundaries of edible creativity even further as I began to create cakes that looked more like sculptures rather than cake (a helicopter, a Gucci handbag, a Porsche, a stack of ornately decorated throw pillows with velvety tassels, even a boxer—just to name a few) and worked with sugar in ways that had clients and their guests believing I'd sculpted an art piece out of glass.

For years, I ran my business as a one-woman show—initially out of the dining room in our two- bedroom apartment in downtown Toronto and then out of the basement of our first house. During those years, I made cakes, pastries, and chocolates for hundreds of birthdays, weddings, and a variety of catering events. As I took on more work, I began to work for high-end catering companies who either didn't do the kind of confectionery work I did or had to farm work out because they were too busy. The work was exciting and creative. However, I was also spending extraordinary amounts of time working weekends, nights, and pulling all-nighters in support of other people's celebrations—often to the point of not being able to attend celebrations of those near and dear to me.

For a while, that was justifiable, even okay. But on the day we celebrated Mylana's second birthday—our backyard filled with family and friends and tonnes of tiny tots laughing, playing, and running around the yard—it occurred to me that I was missing out on so much of my own life. It occurred to me that perhaps it was time for me to do something else.

As I began to seriously talk about leaving the food business, though, a few good friends, one after another, stopped me. "But Lesia," they asked, "do you know how good you are at what you do? Do you have any idea how happy you make people with your edible works of art?" A few of them even said, "If it's time and money that are the issue, let us help you with that."

It didn't take much convincing to realize I actually wasn't done, and that this was my "go big or go home" moment. So, I decided to go big. After ten years in business, I decided to open my dream bakery.

* * *

When I started telling people about my dream, the Universe began to provide. Friends and family invested. My graphic designer connected me to our store designer and with a branding expert, who connected me to a researcher, who connected me to a financial expert, who connected me with my architect and lawyer. One of my friends who invested in the business, attracted more investors and connected me with my first contractor. That first contractor ultimately turned the project over to a more experienced contractor, who in turn led me to the master electrician who ended up being the only tradesperson who worked on the entire project from start to finish. As the project unfolded, the Universe continued to provide.

We were focusing on organic and fair-trade ingredients and a sustainably-minded renovation, consciously endeavouring to minimize our carbon footprint in every area of the business. Our plans and endeavours caught the attention of some local magazines. Articles were written and word began to spread.

The five high-end catering companies I'd been working with for years were excited that I'd finally be able to accommodate larger orders and wrote me glowing letters of support. Those letters of confidence and commitment were partly what ended up helping me to secure big loans from the two big banks that dealt with small businesses. Word continued to spread. Anticipation was in the air.

On November 14, 2008, after a gruelling six-month delay—with our front doors arriving just two hours before our grand opening—LPK's Culinary Groove (LPK's for short) opened its doors.

The journey to our grand opening had been exciting, enlivening, more than slightly scary, and arduous. Yet even with the ups and downs, while working during the entire renovation, we had finally opened, and my dream bakery had come to life. I was thrilled! I felt so incredibly proud of myself and grateful to everyone who had helped to make my dream come true.

I thought, *Looks like I do have what it takes.*

I'd attracted a team of experts and professionals who'd guided me through every step of the process. I'd been backed by friends and family with their investments. We'd hired an amazing staff who were so excited to be part of something so new, so founded in ethical principles, that was also firmly focused on artistry, elegance, and creativity. And then, after the adrenaline rush of celebration felt at our big opening party, we opened our doors the next day.

Almost no one came.

I looked around at my beautiful shop with our mission written on the wall behind the cash desk for all to see. I looked at all these amazing people who had been hired, who were so thrilled to be part of what almost felt like a movement rather than a neighbourhood bakery. I looked at the dismally low number of sales we'd made courtesy of the handful of people who'd walked through our doors, and my heart began to sink. As my heart sank,

I heard my dad's voice once again, "You'll never succeed as an entrepreneur; *you don't have what it takes.*"

Right from the get-go, it was tough. We'd opened just as the global economy tanked and were reminded of it time and time again. The five high-end catering companies I'd been working with for years downsized in big ways so they could survive. People weren't spending money like they had been, and when they were, they weren't spending it on handcrafted, edible luxury chocolate boots and purses that were only an inch tall and cost $7 each (back in 2008). Companies weren't throwing extravagant parties for their staff; they were letting their staff go. The work we'd been promised and the work we'd been counting on had evaporated. And because we were a principled, high-end bakery, offering high-end products, for many, our prices were just...too...high.

The next few months were even tougher. As much as I'd try to lead in an inspirational, "Let's make only what we can sell" and "We're sticking to our principles and that's worth more than money" kind of way, business remained dismal. Although it wasn't part of our business plan, we opened ourselves up to new income streams through wholesaling. It wasn't enough to sustain the business, however, and by late winter, I had to let several of the staff go.

It was hard for everyone. It was hard for those who were let go. It was hard for those who stayed. It was monumentally hard for me after working for so long and so hard to bring this dream to life, to feel like we were drowning after only a few months in.

However, our small but mighty team continued. And with the kindness, generosity, and understanding from some of our lenders, our landlord, and our investors, along with another two injections of financial investment, we managed to keep ourselves afloat—but just barely.

From the outside, LPK's looked beautiful and successful. We garnered media attention, won awards, and were asked to participate in coveted events that championed and promoted sustainability and ethical farming practices. We even had the support of our growing community of friends and fans. On several occasions, they'd answer the call for help sent out via social media.

They came numerous times to help us package thousands of award-winning Spicy Chèvre Noir Shortbread Cookies for massive events. In exchange, they got to hang out in our kitchen after hours, eat delicious organic cakes, pastries, and chocolates, and leave with a gift certificate to spend in our shop neatly tucked in their pockets. Most of all—at least for me—they'd receive my undying gratitude.

We were also becoming more and more recognized, especially after we began actively participating in the local farmers' markets. In addition to garnering attention for our beautiful, delicious cakes, pastries, and chocolates, we were also receiving more attention for our commitment to sustainability and for knowing who and where our food comes from. I remember one foodie event we participated in at Hart House at the University of Toronto, where the founder of a well-known store on the Danforth dedicated to selling only environmentally responsible clothing and household products came up to our table and congratulated me on what we were doing with my bakery. He told me that he knew how hard it was to make and stand by that kind of ethical and environmental commitment and that I should be very proud. I was blown away.

I remember feeling like I'd entered the big leagues of sustainability and the local sustainable food scene when LPK's was asked to participate in Foodstock in 2011—a one-day event spearheaded by famed and revered chef Michael Stadtländer—to raise funds and awareness to stop the destruction of prime farmland in Southern Ontario, which was being threatened by a proposed mega quarry.

The event took place on Stadtländer's farm, with approximately seventy chefs and food artisans each preparing a dish that showcased some of what Southern Ontario had to offer in terms of produce, meat, cheese, bread, and more. The day was filled with music, inspirational and activational speakers, and, of course, food. In an effort to drastically reduce the amount of garbage that could potentially be generated at an event with thousands in attendance, attending foodies were asked to bring their own plates, cutlery, cups, and napkins with them.

I still remember setting up our tent in the forest, with the fall leaves crunching beneath our feet. We hung up our sign, put out our table, and laid out hundreds and hundreds of mini organic, vegan, gluten-free apple crumbles—anticipating we'd be at our table for the better part of the day—and waited.

At 9 a.m., as I looked to my left, there they were. It was as if not one, but several busloads of people were marching toward us with their plates, cutlery, and mugs in hand, ready to partake in what the Foodstock community of chefs and food artisans had whipped up.

If you've ever seen an episode of *The Walking Dead* where a horde descends on a town, you'll know what I felt. An enormous mass of hungry foodies, ready to dig into whatever was in their path, marched purposefully, single-mindedly, closer and closer to our tent, ready to dig into our mini apple crumbles, which featured apples from our friends' farm in Niagara.

Joyfully, enthusiastically, these ethically-minded gourmands devoured the tiny treats we had on offer. After the delightful but short-lived frenzy—in less than just 45 minutes—*every last crumble was gone*. It was thrilling and felt so amazing to be part of such a worthwhile cause while making people so happy at the same time.

However, even though it felt great to be part of an event like this (and others like it), it didn't translate to increased revenue for our business. It was as if you could either be principled and environmentally and community-minded, or you could be financially successful. As the months and years wore on, it became harder and harder to justify keeping the business going.

* * *

One of the biggest costs of running my business was the ceaseless strain and volatility it wrought on my family.

Mylana was only three years old when we began work on the bakery. She was already in a casa class (three- to five-year-olds) at a local Montessori school during the week and in Ukrainian school on Saturdays. Working seven days a week, often pulling one or two all-nighters each week, I'd regularly choose to sleep on the bakery's kitchen floor on a piece of cardboard with my coat as a pillow. In my mind it made sense that if I didn't spend the time travelling back and forth from home, not only could I actually sleep for an hour or two, but I could also "show up" to work earlier and get more done. As a result, I spent very little time at home.

For the four and half years I ran the bakery, Mylana didn't see much of her mom. For all intents and purposes, Glenn became a single parent. For years, many of the kids in Mylana's class (along with their parents) had no idea who Mylana's mom was.

Glenn would also give up his weekends, coming down to the markets with Mylana in tow to help tear down, pack up, and drive me back to the shop, just so I could do it all again the next day. He would also be the one to take Mylana across town to Ukrainian school, where even though pretty much everyone there could speak English, not many would accommodate Glenn. As such, he didn't really understand or know what was going on. After school, Glenn would come home, call my mom in Edmonton, and then muddle through as best he could, trying to interpret instructions and exercises in a language that he didn't speak, just so Mylana could get help with her homework. Even through all of this, I still felt that my business needed me more, and that that's where I belonged.

* * *

Glenn Sheridan is one of the smartest, funniest, kindest, gentlest, most intuitive people I have ever met. And he's got the patience of a saint.

Born in Belfast, Northern Ireland, he emigrated to Canada twice—first, when he was seven and then again when he was sixteen. He's the youngest of seven children, and his eldest sister is just one year younger than my mom.

Glenn is the love of my life and my best friend. I could write an entire book on how blissful I felt when he first held my hand; how sensuous our first kiss was; how thrilling it was when I realized I was pregnant while he lay sleeping quietly next to me; how much I cherish the beautiful poems, cute doodles, and esoteric witticisms he wrote me when we first started dating; how touched I was by the baker's dozen sock bouquet he made me for Valentine's Day one year; how devoted a father he's been; how his love of language, words, and song lyrics fuel and pepper his mind and soul with ever-expanding curiosity, playfulness, and creativity; and how my love of Tom Waits' music opened the door to his heart, which in turn, gave him the key to mine. And yet...

There were several times during the four and a half years of the bakery when our marriage was tested. There was one night when my disregard for our marriage had reached an all-time high, largely thanks to my skewed perception of duty and responsibility to the business.

It was late at night and the bakery had long since closed. I was sitting on the wooden step stool just beneath the phone on the wall in the kitchen, probably telling Glenn for the millionth time that I wouldn't be home that night because I had to work. Although I don't remember exactly what was said, I do remember the pain, suffering, and sheer exhaustion I was feeling—not really being able to tell if it was mine, Glenn's, or a mixture of both. As I rambled on about how important it was for me to stay at the shop, Glenn finally managed to say, "Love, I can't do this anymore. You're breaking my heart."

Even though I could hear the woundedness in his voice, I also heard what I can only describe as resignation. This time, he meant it. He was done. I hung up the phone and thought, *My marriage is over.*

It took a few minutes, and even though I knew I had orders to fill, I also felt the anxiety building in my chest and throat. Glenn was ready to leave me, and I was *still* sitting at the bakery. I didn't know what to do, so I called my friend Laura. Even though she had two small boys of her own and it was late at night, when I told her I thought Glenn and I had just broken up, she dropped everything and came right over.

We sat at the retail table, mostly talking about TV shows. I couldn't talk about how afraid I was of losing Glenn, of what it would mean to not be married anymore. I was so sleep-deprived and overworked, I wasn't even able to fully realize, never mind acknowledge, how much I'd hurt the person I loved the most and how absent I'd been from my young daughter's life. If I even entertained what a colossal failure I'd been as a human being, I would've completely broken down. So we continued our conversation about TV shows for a few hours until I felt better and it was time for Laura to go home to her family. I was so thankful to have someone I could turn to because it seemed like the person that had been mine to turn to for so long was getting ready to let me go.

As the months wore on, even with the help of friends and my mom, reprieves from the banks and our landlord, and the expertise of a consultant who worked with us, the hole I'd dug for myself felt too deep to climb out of. The financial, emotional, and physical burden was too much to bear. All that was left to do was to close it down.

I don't remember the conversations I had with Glenn. I don't even remember the day I decided I was done. It had been a battle of Sisyphean proportions—the proverbial boulder being rolled uphill.

For years I'd tried so many ways to keep the business going, all with little financial success. I was told to "just use cheaper ingredients and materials." People tried to persuade me that, "it doesn't matter about the environment." I was encouraged numerous times to compromise my values and principles and then I'd be able to make money.

What those people didn't seem to understand was that my business wasn't just about our beloved Coconut Lime Cake, the award-winning Nanaimo Bars, the Spicy Chèvre Noir Shortbreads, or the handcrafted, jewel-like chocolates we made. It was about our *mission*. It was about "Delighting our clients by treating them, our ingredients, and our world with love and respect." Using cheaper, unethically made ingredients would not only diminish the brand, but it would also go against our very reason for being!

Unfortunately, even my steadfast commitment to that mission—which was skewed anyway, as I didn't treat my family or myself with much love and respect back then—wasn't enough to sustain and support the business to financial success. Eventually, it came time to tell the staff we were closing.

* * *

I loved my staff. Whether paid kitchen or retail staff member, intern, or volunteer, everyone who walked through our doors was talented, committed, and devoted to their work. Each of them brought their own unique "something" that enriched and elevated the culture of LPK's. They also put up with an enormous amount of volatility and instability from me. I can only imagine what having a driven, committed, but inordinately sleep-deprived boss who was facing financial ruin and seemed to care more about her business than her family must have been like.

Still, this amazing collective of beings worked together, got frustrated together, laughed, even cried together. We celebrated after our big events, and eventually began celebrating Thanksgiving together. A few years after closing the bakery, before our family's move to Victoria, we had our last Thanksgiving dinner in Toronto. I looked at the table with so many of my former staff who were now my friends—amazing beings with their own young and growing families—and my heart filled with gratitude.

When I first told my staff about my decision to close the bakery—through tears of sadness, embarrassment, and an immense sense of loss—everyone was so kind, so loving, so supportive. I wanted to let them know several months in advance, so if they wanted to find other work, they had time to do so. I remember the tears and hugs, and one of them whisper in my ear as she hugged me, "I'll stay with you til the end. We got this, girl." In that moment, I felt a deep sense of relief knowing we could now move forward with our plans.

Over the next several weeks as the news spread, the shock wore off and the reality sunk in that my dream was indeed running its course, the outpouring of love and support from the community, our clients, and our lenders was mind-blowing. People came out in droves, buying what they could to help us pay our suppliers so we could close our doors knowing we had done our best to not let anyone, including our lenders, down. Several customers even bought chest freezers so they could stock up on our organic, vegan, gluten-free treats and have them on hand for months to come.

Some of the staff moved on while some stayed. And together, my dream business was slowly dismantled one day, one order, sometimes one moment, at a time.

We decided to close the retail portion of the bakery on New Year's Eve 2012. We had an open house where we served our well-loved Sweet Potato Doughnuts tossed with local organic maple sugar along with several with other fan favourites.

We laughed, told stories, listened to music, ate, and drank. And then at 8 p.m. (our designated "midnight"), I made a small speech of gratitude. Glenn cued up "For Auld Lang Syne" by The Good Lovelies (a tune on the Canadian band's Christmas album that had been on high rotation throughout the holiday season). We all got in a circle, clasped hands, and danced and sang as we celebrated LPK's Culinary Groove one last time. I can still feel the love, joy, gratitude of that night.

In January 2013, there were just two of us working in the kitchen, doing the work of five. We filled our last orders and tied up loose ends. In that final month, as we worked harder than ever, there was even more music and laughter (thank you "Adam and Joe" and BBC 6 Music). There was even more love.

During that month, some of the staff and our favourite customers-turned-friends came back to help us tear down, pack, and move.

Amidst the stress and surrealistic experience of saying goodbye to what had felt like my reason for being for so many years, I couldn't help but feel grateful *and* sad. I'd lost all the money Glenn and I had, and we were about to sell our home of nearly twelve years—the house where Mylana was born—to cover some of the debt I'd incurred over the past four and a half years. I'd lost every penny of financial investment from family and friends. And I'd lost years of time with Glenn and Mylana and our friends.

Through it all though, I couldn't help but remember all the laughter, the staff lunches, the dancing and singing at the *Green Living Show* while frying up and handing out *thousands* of cones of Sweet Potato Doughnuts. I remember the shock and delight when we were told by one of our customers that famed foodie author Ruth Reichel had just tweeted, "Spicy Chèvre Noir Shortbreads from LPK's. Just ate whole bag on plane."

I also delight in remembering the absolute thrill of winning Vegan Cupcakes Take Over Toronto! at the 2012 Toronto Vegetarian Food Festival. My staff and I spent hours upon hours (with the staff donating their time) creating a series of miniature edible figurines representing the various businesses in our neighbourhood (the library, a strip bar, the hardware store, just to name a few) as we put together an edible journey of our Riverside neighbourhood on display. We showcased our famed Coconut Lime Cupcakes and our specially made Double Chocolate Fudge, Ganache-Filled with Caramelized Popcorn Cupcakes, beating out what many touted as our main competition—a nationwide company dedicated to producing vegan and gluten-free prepared desserts.

And then, on January 31, 2013, that was it. LPK's Culinary Groove closed its doors for good. My dream bakery was gone, and I had no idea what I was going to do next.

* * *

The matter most pressing was selling our house. Even though I'd amassed hundreds of thousands of dollars of debt, because there was equity in our home, we weren't able to declare bankruptcy. As such, we had to sell our beloved home to offset the debt.

Glenn and I had put so much heart and soul into that house as we'd built our home and life together for over a decade. The fact that Mylana had been born there, at the side of our bed, surrounded by our birthing village made up of my mom, our doula, naturopath, and midwives—with our neighbours outside eagerly awaiting the first glimpse of this tiny creature that had been growing in my belly for the past nine months—made it that much harder to let go. But let go we had to and let go we did.

The next couple of months went by quickly and there were numerous times I didn't know if I had what it took to get through them. We were in the middle of this extraordinary upheaval because I'd failed. Even though we eventually found a new home (which did feel like a fresh start), all of this trauma and volatility was compounded by me feeling that without my bakery, without my work, I no longer had a purpose. I literally had no idea what to do with myself. Further compounding my feelings of ineffectualness were the confusion and frustration that came with me not knowing how to cope with my dad's cancer diagnosis and the fact that he was back in my life.

For months, I'd thought that when the bakery finally closed and we'd said goodbye to our home, I would feel better because the worst was over. But I was wrong.

* * *

We moved into our new home (a rental) in March, and within weeks, I began to panic. Glenn would go to work, Mylana would go to school, and I'd be home alone, not knowing what to do, becoming more and more anxious. I started to exercise and take better care of myself, thinking the anxiety would dissipate. I tried immersing myself in housework, thinking that if I created a lovely home, perhaps I would find peace and purpose in that. I thought if I just hung around and gave myself time to do nothing, without having any kinds of expectations, I'd soon be able to work through the gamut of emotions that were coming up, amplifying and concretizing what now felt like the most epic failure of my life.

Without work, I felt useless. Feeling useless reminded me of how much damage I'd done to my family and to my health and how I'd disappointed so many who'd believed in me. I felt so ashamed. All I wanted to do was make up for all the pain and disappointment I'd caused and to one day, maybe be able to pay back my friends and family the money they'd invested in my business—in *me*.

I became so distraught that one day, sobbing, I called my friend Seema. Like Laura had done many months before, Seema dropped what she was doing, drove over, and sat with me on my living room couch, holding me as the tears flowed and the sadness and confusion poured out.

She sat and listened. In that moment, she was my friend, my mom, my older sister—she was the embodiment of kindness and compassion.

"Oh Lesia, you've gone through so much. You just need someone to hold you and let you cry. You need to feel everything." And then she said, "You're grieving."

Grieving? How could I be grieving? No one had died.

The truth was, however, I had lost something—my bakery. The closing of my bakery was the end of a vibrant dream come to life—the business I had so often referred to as my first baby. All of that was gone, yes. The sadness was overwhelming, all-consuming, and profound. But it was also so much more than that.

The guilt and shame that had been hanging around for months as I came to terms with the financial failure of the bakery were now looming—massive albatrosses hovering over my head and taking up space in my mind. I could barely breathe. The suffocating weight of failure wasn't just about losing my bakery, it was about my failure at being a person, of just *being*. It was me failing at life, period.

I was grieving—not only for LPK's—but also for myself. Somewhere along the way, I had become so consumed with the bakery, I'd completely lost myself in the process. Now, without the bakery and my work to anchor me, I felt completely untethered in the worst way imaginable. It was as if I were free-falling into the unknown, trying desperately to grasp hold of something, *anything*, as I careened aimlessly into the abyss below. It was one of the scariest feelings I've ever experienced, and even though I was being held by one of my closest friends, I'd also never felt so alone.

In the coming weeks and months (years really), I surfed the gamut of feelings and emotions as I tried to make sense of what had happened. I tried desperately to figure out why this amazing dream—which had so much passion and drive and enthusiasm behind it—had failed after such a short time. I knew I'd made the right decision in closing it down, but for a long, *long* time after closing our doors, I still couldn't believe things had unfolded the way they had.

I'd ask myself over and over again, *Why weren't our signature Myloreos, Sweet Potato Doughnuts, Coconut Lime Cake, Spicy Chèvre Noir Shortbreads, Chocolate Chip Sandwich Cookies, and Nanaimo Bars enough? Why weren't our values and principles enough? Why wasn't I enough?*

The same feelings of inadequacy that had plagued me during my childhood and young adulthood bubbled back up to the surface. Every aspect of my post-LPK's life seemed to be a reminder of me *"not having what it takes"* to be an entrepreneur and that, ultimately, I *wasn't* good enough—just like the voice in my head I'd kept hearing over the years.

As the guilt, shame, and anger continued to grow, so did the desire to make up for what I'd done. After only a few months of grieving, I dove back into the farmers' markets, once again as a one-woman show, just so I could generate some income for my family. And because I'd left on such good terms with everyone, I was welcomed back with open arms.

It didn't take long to realize, though, I really didn't want to be there. Being at the markets themselves was great. Being outdoors, seeing my old clients, hanging with the organic farmers and food artisans who'd become my friends, even having old clients come and help out at my stall—all of that was amazing! What wasn't so great was the hours I'd spend getting ready for these markets, with Glenn going back to giving up his weekends in order to help me because I was so exhausted after working all night and it wasn't safe for me to drive.

Eventually, I made the decision to leave the food business for good, even choosing which farmers' market season would be my last. The interesting thing was that when that happened, I found myself drawn to the world of integrative nutrition health coaching. And because I'd already been working with so many different diets and lifestyles for years as I accommodated my clients, health coaching seemed like the next obvious step on this new trajectory.

* * *

The next two years felt like a mixed bag. Just as I started my integrative nutrition health coaching program (which was super exciting), my dad died. His death was just as unsettling as the moment he came back into my life over two years earlier.

After taking some time, I caught up with and worked my way through school and was finally beginning to let go of the recent past. Soon, I found myself feeling extremely grateful, with a newfound sense of freedom. To celebrate, I wanted to do something for my family, including my mom, as a way of saying thank you. *Thank you for supporting me. Thank you for putting up with me. Thank you for not giving up on me.*

In the summer of 2014, we decided to take a two-week vacation. We would fly to Edmonton, where my mom still lived, and then road-trip our way through the Rockies, eventually making our way to Victoria to spend a week with my sister and her family. Because my expenses had diminished significantly since closing the bakery, I'd actually been able to make some money, setting aside enough to pay for our vacation—in advance.

One day, during the planning of our trip, I had the very distinct feeling that during our trip, we'd make the decision to move to Victoria. I didn't say anything to anybody—not even Glenn. I just *knew* —in my heart and soul—this was something that was going to happen.

Chapter 3

A Leap of Faith

"He still had some doubts about the decision he had made. But he was able to understand one thing: making a decision was only the beginning of things. When someone makes a decision, he is really diving into a strong current that will carry him to places he had never dreamed of when he first made the decision."
— Paulo Coelho, *The Alchemist*

On a sizzling August morning, Glenn and I had just completed an invigorating and breathtaking two-hour climb up Mount Finlayson (about twenty minutes outside of Victoria, British Columbia) with my sister, Larissa, and my nephew. Exhilarated and exhausted, we were drenched in sweat.

As we walked past the sparsely populated arbutus and Garry oak trees and the odd shrubbery, we found a clear, relatively flat spot on the rocks and collapsed. Nearby, a black-and-yellow butterfly gently rested on a stone from which a tiny purple flower grew. As we allowed ourselves to melt into the ground beneath us, our breathing slowly returned to normal. Above us, in clear blue skies, eagles and falcons soared so close we could almost touch them. Before us was the most extraordinary panorama of trees, mountains, and ocean as far as the eye could see. The sun beat down with its energy and warmth. Hummingbirds flitted to and fro. I felt grateful to be alive. I thought, *Life couldn't possibly get any better than this.*

As we lay there, soaking in the intoxicating deliciousness of our surroundings—our senses bedazzled, our souls awakened and inspired—I don't even remember who said it first, but somehow, out of one of our mouths came, *"What would it take to make this our life? What would we have to do to get here?"*

* * *

In the summer of 2013, filled with exuberance and a newfound sense of freedom, we started planning our vacation.

Our daughter Mylana was turning ten the following year, and except for the odd two- or three-day getaway to Great Wolf Lodge in Niagara Falls, we'd never taken a family vacation. Although one of the reasons had been due to a lack of available funds for anything other than regular life and business expenses, the main reason for not having taken a family vacation had really been due to lack of time. Or rather, me being utterly convinced I couldn't be away from my business for more than a day or two, or my business would fall apart.

I was convinced my clients would forget about me and turn to another supplier. I believed I'd stop bringing in what little money I was making, and I'd be even more of a burden to my family than I already had been. For years, I'd put my business first and everyone and everything else second, third, tenth, etc. As a result, over a decade had gone by without us ever having taken a proper family vacation and without me having taken any significant time away from work.

I also wanted to do something nice for my mom; like, really nice. I wanted to give her the gift of a vacation—one where she didn't have to pay for anything.

After my mom left my dad, I was angry with her for years. I couldn't understand why she'd left. I made up stories in my mind as to why. I blamed her for breaking up our family. I blamed her for making me choose which parent to live with. I blamed her for leaving me, further instilling the notion that I wasn't good enough. If I had been, she would've insisted that I live with her.

In my early twenties, my mom and I found our way back to each other. My summer Edmonton visits, her fall and/or Christmastime Toronto visits, and the weekly epic long-distance calls in between melted away the anger and blame that had been the foundation for our relationship for several years. Once I got my mom back, I also felt like I'd made a new bestie—a girlfriend I could be totally honest with, laugh, cry, and gossip with—who loved and supported me no matter what I said or did.

I know she's my mom and she's supposed to love and support me, but I felt she'd been over-the-top generous in so many ways throughout my adult life. And not just with the big things, like buying a house, or investing in my business, but with the smaller things, like all the dinners and groceries she'd pay for when she came to visit, or when I'd go to Edmonton to visit her. Or all the times she'd say, "Here's some money to buy some gaz," (her way of pronouncing the word *gas*). Or all the times we'd go window shopping for her and I'd make her buy herself something nice, but then she'd see me eyeing something and say, "Do you like that? Why don't I get it for you as an early birthday present?" It could've been January—my birthday is in October.

The point is, I wanted to treat my mom for a change while doing something fun for my family. So over the next year, we planned, and saved, and planned some more.

We decided it'd be fun to do a road trip from Edmonton, through the mountains via Vancouver, ending up in Victoria, where my sister lived. We'd fly into Edmonton (where I grew up and where my mom still lives) and then drive with my mom through Calgary into the mountains, passing through Banff and then stopping for a few days in Radium Hot Springs and surrounding area along the way.

Radium and the neighbouring town of Invermere hold special places in my heart, and in my mom's. During many summers while growing up, my parents, my sister, and I, along with my grandparents and maybe some of our cousins and my great aunt, would head west into the Rockies to the tiny tourist town of Radium Hot Springs to spend a few days soaking in the hot, mineral-rich, mountain water—a decades-old tradition on my mom's side of the family. We'd stay in these tiny, cheap, no-frills, one-room motels, often in a unit neighbouring our baba and dido (my grandparents).

I remember Larissa and I waking up early, sneaking over to knock on our grandparents' door so we could have breakfast in their room. Unlike our parents, my baba and dido had those tiny little cereal packs you could tear open along the little perforated lines, magically turning the tiny box of forbidden Frosted Flakes, Rice Krispies, or Raisin Bran into a delightful bowl of morning deliciousness and fun. Back in our room, it was just boring old Shreddies or oatmeal.

With coolers of snacks my parents and grandparents had packed, we'd head on over to the hot springs for a morning and early-afternoon soak and swim, with the occasional soft-serve ice cream treat from the takeout cafeteria above and a siesta in between. Our evenings would be filled with walks around town, games of canasta with my grandparents and great aunt, and the odd drive-in movie. Every now and then, we might even venture over to Fairmont Hot Springs—the fancy resort about twenty minutes further down the highway.

So, how comforting and what a joy it was for my mom and me to feel like we'd stepped back in time as we arrived in Radium in August of 2014. I'd booked us an amazing-looking two-bedroom condo. Much to our delight, our reservation ended up being upgraded to a four-bedroom that was fully equipped with all the comforts of home (except for a fine-mesh strainer, which I had to go out and buy), ensuring a lovely, relaxing stay in a little corner of the world that held so many amazing memories for me, even more so for my mom.

We spent a few days in Radium and the nearby towns of Fairmont and Invermere. We basked in the fresh mountain air, luxurious mineral-rich hot springs, were entertained by the mountain goats nimbly frolicking on the rocky edges of the cliffs around us and marvelled at the deer that just casually walked the town streets in the middle of the day, grazing on people's lawns without a seeming care in the world. And when it came to siesta time, Glenn and Mylana would take turns napping in the different bedrooms, just because they could.

After a few days, we made our way through to Golden and over to Vancouver. We spent a couple of days with good friends, dipping our toes in the Pacific Ocean (Glenn's and Mylana's very first time). We visited the various kiosks and artists' studios on Granville Island and dined at an amazing restaurant. Glenn, my mom, and I also had the opportunity to briefly dig into the mysteries and history showcased at the Museum of Anthropology. Then we hopped the ferry to Vancouver Island, where my sister greeted us with smiles, open arms, and massive hugs.

As the second half of our vacation unfolded, what was initially a fleeting thought a few months earlier (and then an overt question as Glenn and I lay on the rocks at the top of Mount Finlayson), eventually presented itself as such a strong pull, we could not help but answer the call. *"What would it take to make this our life? What would we have to do to get here?"*

During dinner after the Mount Finlayson climb, we began seriously talking about what life could look like if we moved from Toronto to Victoria. We had no idea what it would take to make it happen, and at that point, it didn't matter. We were completely thrilled, enraptured, and inspired by this new dream of creating a better, more fulfilling, and vibrant life on the West Coast.

By the end of our holiday, Glenn, my sister, my mom, and I were so excited! Glenn could once again live near the ocean (something he missed since leaving his homeland of Northern

Ireland decades earlier). Larissa and I would be back together again after decades of living on different continents and opposite sides of the country.

Larissa and I talked about getting together once a week for family dinners and to just hang out. She also offered to pick Mylana up from school on Fridays so they could get to know each other better. If Glenn didn't find a job right away, he could work with Larissa's husband until he found work. My mom would have both her daughters and all of her grandkids in one place—no more travelling to Toronto during either smog-infested, hot, and humid summers, or frigid and filthy winters. And I could continue along the path I'd just embarked on as an integrative nutrition health coach.

Because Mylana would be graduating grade six in two years and would be switching schools anyway, we decided the summer of 2016 would be the perfect time to move. It felt like everything was coming together so easily, and it felt thrilling to be inspired in such an activational way. This idea also seemed to make so many around me super excited and delighted, too.

When we got back to Toronto a week later, we began announcing to our friends, "We're moving to Victoria!" And even though some initially asked why or didn't really believe we'd go through with it, we began planning, saving, and planning some more.

* * *

For the next two years, we planned, scheduled, saved, and got ready for our cross-country move. We even went back to Victoria the following year to tour some Montessori schools just in case Mylana wanted to continue with Montessori rather than going to public school. I also hosted a wellness workshop at my sister's and attended a networking event with an acquaintance of hers, all in an effort to start connecting with people in advance.

Back in Toronto, I began to wind down my food business and even started looking for someone who might be interested in taking over my catering business. There was one big company that that was very keen to get their hands on some of my most-prized recipes, but after a few months of talks and negotiations, it wasn't a good fit for all involved and, ultimately, I let that opportunity go.

What I really wanted was to hand the business over to someone who would value it as much as I had. I wanted to hand it over to someone who would take care of my beloved clients and fans as I had for years. I wanted to pass the proverbial torch (or spatula, as it were) to someone who'd continue to make my Nanaimo Bars along with other fan favourites like the Chocolate Chip Sandwich Cookie, Myloreo, and Sourdough Rice Buns and Focaccia that had people coming to my home to purchase them after the bakery had closed. I wanted someone to keep delighting my clients by treating them, our ingredients, and our world with love and respect.

There were a few individuals I thought of and approached, but no one was in a position to buy a business at that time. One couple was even thinking of getting out of the food and farming business entirely, thinking it might be time for them to retire.

In an interesting turn of events, though, the farming couple, who also owned and operated a beautiful bakery in a small town about 100 km east of Toronto, ended up deciding they did want to get into the organic, gluten-free, plant-based dessert and baked goods business after all. So we ended up negotiating a deal that seemed fair for everyone. I really felt that these people were the perfect people to take over my business and keep taking care of my beloved clients.

Eventually, I stopped working and began to focus on our move full time. There was packing, finding a place to live in a city we barely knew, and continuing to connect with some of the people I'd met the summer before. There was also driving to the bakery in the small town 100 km outside of Toronto several times a week to train the main staff member in how to properly make my signature desserts and baked goods—to the point that customers could eventually come to a market table or a supermarket pastry counter and *immediately* recognize their favourite sweets and treats, even if they appeared under a new brand name.

It meant an extraordinary number of hours of work and extra driving for weeks. However, I was determined to give this couple and their business, along with what had been my first baby nearly two decades earlier, the most rock-solid foundation for continued success.

As we got closer and closer to our departure date, however, I found myself starting to get very antsy. I started wondering, *What are we doing?* and *Why are we leaving a perfectly good life in Toronto?*

Even on those days, I felt sure we were doing the "right thing," finding myself tasked with getting rid of 75 percent of our stuff, finding a place to live, and dismantling my business *again* led to overwhelming anxiety and apprehension about our impending move.

I thought I might be making the wrong decision and that I might be leading my family into another debacle, not unlike LPK's—a wound that was healing but still felt rather tender in mind, heart, and soul.

One day, I was on the verge of completely unravelling and freaking out and I called my mom. As the tears streamed down my face and anxiety shook my voice, I told her that being surrounded by moving boxes, packing peanuts, and packing tape with no one to help me was making me crazy and I didn't know where to begin. In true mama fashion she asked, "Le, do you want me to come down and help you pack?" With utmost gratitude and relief in my heart I said, "Yes, please."

Once my mom arrived, things got easier, and I found a rhythm. We were well on our way to saying thank you and goodbye to nearly three decades of adult life in Toronto and the only life Mylana had ever known.

* * *

When we were ready to look for a new place to live, I arranged with my sister (who'd lived in Victoria for nearly a decade by that point) to check out potential places on our behalf. As we started the house-hunting process, we noticed almost immediately that rents were significantly higher in Victoria than in Toronto, and most didn't include utilities. And, unlike in Ontario where tenants are required to give sixty days' written notice to terminate a rental agreement, in British Columbia, it was only thirty days.

We were ready for the West Coast, but the West Coast wasn't quite ready for us. Little did we also know that the vacancy rate in Victoria was *less than 0.5 percent.*

When I eventually started finding places, I made appointments for Larissa to go and check them out. Along with a list of preferred criteria for our new home, my sister was under strict instructions to have "the package" with her wherever she went.

"The package" was a set of documents Glenn and I had put together to show prospective landlords that we'd be stellar tenants. Our credit rating was in the toilet thanks to the failure of my bakery, and we were paying off our debt until May 2019. We felt confident that the contents within would prove to landlords we were worth the risk.

There were letters of recommendation from our current landlord, Glenn's boss of nearly twenty years, and a few of my clients, along with financial information showing we had money in the bank to pay first and last month's rent. We also had the proposal details along with a glowing recommendation from our bankruptcy trustee who'd filed and guided us through the proposal process. And just for good measure—as suggested by a close friend of ours—we included a family photo, so that landlords could also see that we were a lovely, trustworthy, and responsible family.

It took less than a week, however, to feel like potential homes in our new land were evaporating through our fingers. No sooner would I make a viewing appointment, than I'd receive an email or a phone call from the realtor, agent, or landlord saying, "We just rented the unit. You can tell your sister not to come."

As properties got snapped up before my eyes, the exorbitant rents also made us question whether we could really afford to live there. Some realtors politely suggested that we might want to increase our budget or lower our expectations. One realtor even wrote that there was *no way* we'd ever find what we wanted within the price range we had in mind. It was impossible, and we were living in a fantasy world. *Welcome to Victoria…*

As far as our Toronto life was concerned, we were already on our way out the door. As for our new Victoria life, however, the only thing sorted so far was that Mylana was enrolled in her new school. Other than that, we had no jobs, no community to speak of, and nowhere to live.

Even as panic started to set in, we were convinced there was a place for us and we just had to keep looking. After all, it felt like we were being called to move across the country. And if the Universe was indeed nudging us to take this extraordinary leap of faith, surely the Universe wouldn't want us to be homeless.

Within days, a whole bunch of new properties popped up. However, as soon as I found them, an email or a voice on the other end of the phone would say something like, "Oh, sorry, the unit was rented this morning. We forgot to change the ad."

Until that one phone call.

* * *

As I combed the internet for more vacancies, I found an ad for a unit that appeared to be on the same street as Mylana's new school. It was a brand-new listing. Upon calling the number, however, I was told, "Sorry, the unit is all but rented." Just as I was ready to hang up the phone, the kind voice on the other end said, "Tell me your story."

So, I told the voice on the other end the story of our road trip two years earlier. I told her about my incredibly strong, secret feeling about moving to Victoria. I told her about the loss of my bakery only a few years earlier and how the subsequent proposal left us with a nonexistent credit rating, making it that much harder to come across as suitable tenants. I told her about how we'd planned this move for two years, felt so ready and willing to embark on this new adventure, even having a school set up for our daughter, Mylana, only to feel like we were coming up short in terms of finding a place to live.

After all that, even though the unit was virtually rented, the kind voice on the other end said, "You know what? Why doesn't your sister come and see the place anyway? We also have a unit on the main floor that won't be ready until September and perhaps that might work." The unit sounded like it could work, but not necessarily within our time frame or budget.

Still, there was something about her voice, her willingness to listen to my story, and the connection that had just been made. So, I agreed to have my sister go look. I hung up, called Larissa, and told her what had happened. I asked her to have "the package" at the ready and to call this woman to make an appointment.

A few hours later, my sister met with the landlord. Right away, she knew the lower unit wouldn't work. When she took a look at the upstairs unit, however, Larissa discovered that most of the renovation work left was cosmetic, which meant it could be done while someone was living there. After a brief discussion, the landlord agreed.

My sister called me from her car and said, "Le, you have to take the upstairs unit. It's perfect for you guys! The landlord is amazing! You're going to love her!"

Ready to burst with glee, I asked, "Did you give her the package?" To which she replied, "Of course!" I was to call the landlord a few hours later after she'd had time to go through "the package" and confer with her husband.

Later that evening, I ducked out in the middle of a screening of *The Nice Guys* to make the all-important phone call. While the Victoria landlord watched one of her kids play soccer, I covered my ear from all the extraneous noise at the cinema.

Within minutes, she decided that, based on our conversation, having met my sister, and the feeling she had—*without even looking at the contents of "the package"*—Glenn, Mylana, and I would make great tenants. She said she and her husband would gladly rent the upstairs unit to us, offering it at a lower rate that would match the rent we'd set as our ceiling. And as long as we were okay with them finishing up their renovations after we moved in, we could move in on August 7th, the day before our Toronto belongings were due to arrive.

Huzzah! The Universe really *did* have our backs! And as it turned out, we could even see Mylana's new school from the front door.

* * *

In the weeks before we left, we had an epic moving sale that brought our neighbours—many of whom we were meeting for the first time—out in droves. As folks walked from section to section of the sale (yes, we had everything organized and laid out according to the "department" it might fall under in an actual store), picking up anything from a bunch of books to used planters to toys and housewares to office and patio furniture and more, it was amazing and so satisfying to see the stuff that represented decades of Glenn's, Mylana's, and my life be dispersed and scattered to the wind. It was equally gratifying to see all of our old things being welcomed into new homes and new lives. It was so comforting and heartwarming to watch our neighbours set up the patio furniture that had been ours just hours earlier on their deck, already breaking bread, sharing stories, and giving this furniture a new life in their home.

Over the next few weeks, we said goodbye to our friends. Mylana had her last Toronto birthday party and sleepover. We were thrown a massive going-away party, organized by three of our closest friends, which ended up bringing all of our worlds together—my former staff, people from the farmers' markets, our spiritual community, Glenn's workmates, friends, and family. What an absolute joy it was to eat, drink, laugh, tell stories, and dance together. What an absolute delight it was to celebrate our love and friendship with all of these amazing people who had become our community—our chosen family—during our time in Toronto.

Our furniture left a week before we did, so our last week in Toronto was spent staying with two of our favourite friends and their two extraordinary young girls. How lovely and comforting it felt to be welcomed into their home and be part of their young family for a week. And then, early in the morning on July 26, 2016, Mylana and I headed west. Glenn stayed behind a few days longer to attend his niece's wedding and to tie up remaining loose ends.

* * *

How exciting, exhilarating, and bittersweet it was to see our driveway, our home, our life disappear in the rear-view mirror as we began our journey, with Blue Belle (our brand-spankin'- new, cobalt-blue Ford Flex) filled with luggage, houseplants, food, and anticipation for this next chapter of our lives.

A couple of hours into our trip, with the last specks of Hogtown an insinuation on the horizon behind us, I began to relax. No more packing. No more moving. No more goodbyes. With only one task at hand—to get us to Victoria—I was free to let go of the past, trust the future, and be fully present for this part of our journey.

We allowed ourselves ten days to drive across Canada, staying only one night in most cities—just enough time to rest and keep driving the following day. Thunder Bay, Winnipeg, and Edmonton were the exceptions. We also budgeted spending money for food and extras every day, allowing ourselves to splurge on little gifts for ourselves, each other, and our new home.

The first week, clear blue skies and beautiful summer weather greeted us all the way. We followed weaving and winding roads bordered by a bizarre blend of deciduous and coniferous trees growing out of cliffs and gargantuan rock formations. Highlighted by the vast, sparkling, deep blue waters of Lake Superior, the drive through Northern Ontario remains some of the most stunning and captivating countryside I have ever seen.

We stopped at trading posts and tourist attractions and even discovered a tiny shop where we indulged in the most delicious creamy, decadent homemade fudge we'd ever had. *And I'm not even a huge fudge fan.*

One thing I loved about driving through that area of Canada was all of the inukshuks that lined both sides of the highway. Whether on the edge of a cliff, at the base of a century-old pine tree or placed carefully on a boulder the size of our car, hundreds, if not thousands of these tiny little rock formations pointed east and west for kilometres on end.

Eager to join the community of way-showers, Mylana and I pulled over and stopped on the side of the road. We added our own inukshuk contribution to that portion of the Trans-Canada Highway, doing our part to help others navigate their way through the vast Canadian countryside. It was more symbolic than anything, as the main highway is pretty easy to follow. Still, it's nice to think we left our mark somewhere along the way.

Once we hit Manitoba, with its straight, endless roads and seemingly infinite sprawling fields, we recalled friends had warned us that, at that point, the trip would get boring, but I didn't think so in the least. There's something intrinsically awesome and profound about being able to look at voluminous, multi-textured clouds strewn across a never-ending sky over land that seems to go on forever and ever and ever.

Then there were the lush, green rolling hills and valleys, thunderous storm clouds, and pristinely sectioned farmland of Saskatchewan (which reminded Glenn of Ireland). After that, there were the bright blue skies and brilliant yellow fields of canola and wheat in Alberta.

And finally, there were the Rockies, with their majestic reach to the north and south of the Canada/US border, extending from Alberta into British Columbia—our final destination.

Near the end of our pilgrimage, we found ourselves first in line on the ferry from Vancouver to Victoria. The ferry pulled up to the dock and stopped. Even before the safety barrier was released, I had this overwhelming feeling of, *I'm home.* And then, as we drove off the ferry onto Vancouver Island "soil," I felt such exhilaration, such gratitude, such joy to finally, finally, *finally* be where my heart had been for the better part of the past two years.

* * *

We pulled up to our new home and were greeted by our new landlord. Smiles and hugs for everyone! The woman whom I'd only known as the kind, compassionate voice on the other end of the phone was standing in front of me. She and her husband were still working feverishly on some of the final touches of the renovation of our unit but took time out to greet and welcome us.

How remarkable it felt to have travelled over 3,000 km to this brand-spankin'-new chapter of our lives.

A few weeks later, my mom headed back to Edmonton. Then, for the first time in over a month, Glenn, Mylana, and I sat together—just the three of us—and thought, *"Now what?"*

* * *

There had been many challenges that had come up during the time leading up to our departure. Many of them had to do with money and unforeseen expenses—expenses that ate their way into the savings we'd built up over the past couple of years that were meant to keep us going for a few months after we landed on the West Coast. However, none of them compared to the challenge of starting our new life once we'd arrived.

With only a place to live and a school for our daughter, it was time to find/create work, bring in an income, and settle into our new life. Even though in our hearts we knew this was where we were meant to be right now, once the dreamy romanticism of our epic decision to move from Toronto to Victoria started to wear off in the light of day, Glenn and I found ourselves wondering what to do.

For two years we had planned, decluttered, tied up loose ends, and looked forward to embracing and building a new life on Vancouver Island. For two years, I had looked forward to cleaner air, more nature, and spending time getting to know my sister—it had been nearly twenty years since we'd lived in the same city. I had looked forward to less hustle and bustle and a renewed sense of self. For two years, I'd had a project to work on—to get us to Victoria. Now that we had arrived, I didn't know what to do. There was an abundance of clean air, we were immersed in nature, and there was definitely less of pretty much everything one would find in Toronto (traffic, noise, construction, pollution, people, and so on, and so forth).

When it came to my sister, Larissa, and me, however, suddenly, the reality looked very different from the dream. My sister had her own life. At this point in time, she and her husband were building a new home on a property they'd recently bought. And because they'd sold their previous home before having a new one to move into, they too were living in a lovely, but cramped rental for the time being.

Larissa also worked full time and was mom to two amazing kids. It didn't take long to realize that, even with the best of intentions, my sister's life didn't really have much room for us at that time. And for me, although my sister and I had woven in and out of each other's lives throughout most of our adult years, with the most recent "in" being during the year before our dad died, now was beginning to feel a lot more like an "out."

I loved her and wanted to get to know her better. However, just like I'd had in Toronto, she had her friends and her chosen family here. And just because she and I were related by blood, didn't automatically mean that we would suddenly become thick as thieves.

I totally got it, but it made me feel incredibly sad and somewhat heartbroken, nonetheless. For all the talk of weekly family dinners, of us hanging out on a regular basis, of her and Mylana getting to know each other better—*none of it* was happening. And truth be told, I felt let down and disappointed.

We had another friend who'd moved to Victoria from Toronto about fifteen years earlier. Although she'd been super helpful and so supportive when we first arrived, something similar happened with her. She had her own life with her own friends. Just because we were new and didn't know anyone else, didn't mean we were automatically going to become part of her life—just because we lived in the same city once again.

We also had one other set of friends—a super-cool, fun, artistic couple whom we'd known for years and loved spending time with in Toronto. They spent half their time out East, and half on the West Coast, and we were so looking forward to spending more time with them out here. However, the day we were going to meet up with them, something happened—which I still don't understand—and we never reconnected after that. The few people we knew in this new land, friends and family we'd so looked forward to spending more time with, just didn't have time for us. I felt gutted and alone.

* * *

One day, a few months before we left Toronto, Glenn turned to me and said, "You know what I want to do next weekend? I'd like to check out the Centre for Spiritual Living (Toronto)." I wasn't working the farmers' markets anymore and my Sundays were free. So, I said, "Sure." I had been to the Centre a couple of years earlier after one of my employees had suggested I go. Even though the message sounded intriguing, and the community was very vibrant and engaged at the time, it wasn't for me. This time, however, I was up for it.

From the moment we walked in, I instantly felt at home, like I belonged. I had found my peeps. We were greeted with open arms, smiles, and a genuine feeling of "We're so glad you're here!" I also immediately recognized several of my customers as members.

From the opening meditation to the power talk (a five-minute inspirational mini-sermon at the beginning of Sunday Celebration given by one of the licensed spiritual practitioners) to the live band that made us get up and dance to the soul-stirring main talk given by then spiritual director Rev. Jonathan Zenz, my mind was blown completely open, and my heart filled with enthusiasm and delight.

I'd already been listening to and reading Wayne Dyer for several months. Thanks to him, I'd also turned to the teachings of Louise Hay, Bruce Lipton, and Eckhart Tolle. Each of them—using slightly different language—talked about how innately powerful we all are and that we are the ones creating our reality, not the other way around. They talked about one Universal Energy, Spirit, or Source—some even used the word "God"—and how when we allow ourselves to tap into that Universal Power there is no limit to what we can do, how we can live, and who we can become. They also talked about how, in fact, we can tap into that Universal Energy at any time, just by using our minds—by how we think.

However, it wasn't until that Sunday at the Centre (CSL for short)—when I was introduced to the Science of Mind philosophy through Rev. Jonathan and the rest of the CSL Toronto community—I began to understand how truly powerful I might be. To realize I was the creator of my life experience, not someone or something else, was unbelievably empowering for me. This revelation also came at the perfect time. We were already giving up the life we had in Toronto in order to create the new life we desired in Victoria.

The discovery of this community also brought me back to being present for the remaining months we had left in Toronto. I felt so grateful to find something that made me feel happy "to be here now" rather than long for my new life in Victoria. I also felt incredibly excited and inspired to have my mind opened to new possibilities. This community and the Science of Mind teachings are also what opened the door to a new path and the calling that has kept me immersed in spiritual/consciousness studies to this day.

* * *

Knowing there was a Centre for Spiritual Living in Victoria was a relief. Even though the various Centres across the world aren't necessarily related to one another and can have a very different personality (much of that having to do with the spiritual director), they do share a common philosophy and focus on the same tenets. So, before we left Toronto, I wrote a letter of introduction to the minister of CSL Victoria, letting her know that we were on our way.

I was so excited when I received her response of delight and enthusiasm, including an invitation to come to her home for dinner. I was giddy at the thought of continuing the family tradition of hangin' with clergy from the local "church" embodied by my grandmother, great-aunt, two of my mom's cousins, and my mom.

The first time we went to a Sunday Celebration at CSL Victoria, we were welcomed with open arms, smiles, love, and hugs. There was so much excitement as this new, young family from CSL Toronto arrived in Victoria. Still, as lovely as it was, it wasn't our centre back home, and I found myself missing our friends, our community, and our life in Toronto.

One Sunday in September we got up, got ready, and headed down to the Centre. We got there early to help with setup—me with the volunteer greeters, and Glenn, with equipment and seating. As had become part of our routine, Mylana would say hello to whoever was there and would then find a cozy, out-of-the-way spot and settle in with a book or her iPad.

As the sound check ended, the early birds began to arrive and were ushered in for morning meditation. I remained in the foyer, greeting the rest of the members as they arrived.

After meditation, the doors opened, everyone went in. Hellos, hugs, laughter, celebration, life.

As the clock approached 11 a.m., I got my phone to set it up for live streaming Rev. Carrie Hunter's Sunday talk. I noticed there was a message waiting for me from one of my oldest friends from Edmonton. I was so excited to hear from him because it only happened once in a blue moon. That and hearing from someone who'd known me before Victoria felt incredibly grounding and uplifting in the moment. And then...

* * *

I don't remember ever having my knees literally buckle, the way they do in a movie when someone receives devastating, life-shattering news. The message was brief and began with an apology for it not being the best way to let me know. It went on to say that Friday, our mutual friend (his best friend since high school) had committed suicide. Holding my phone, in the midst of the hustle and bustle just before Sunday Celebration at the Centre, I felt complete and utter shock and disbelief. I ran outside, fell to my knees, and sobbed.

Pretty much every time I'd go back to Edmonton, I would make time to see my friend. He was one of the most brilliant, clever, and curious people I had ever met, and he held such a special place in my heart. I so looked forward to our visits. Whether we played pool, went for tea, or I had the pleasure of having lunch at his home and spending time with the three loves of his life—his fiancée and two teenage daughters—every time I hung out with him, he made me think and talk about stuff I wouldn't normally talk about. I would learn so much from him—just by listening, just by being in his company.

He introduced me to Tom Waits, Elvis Costello, The Pogues, and Nick Cave. He loved to dance. He came to visit us in Toronto one year and was bedazzled by a one-year-old Mylana. The following year, he showed up at my baba's funeral, not because he'd known her, but because I'd asked him to.

He'd also written a children's book many years earlier—a story I didn't appreciate until decades later after I'd become a mom. *I'm so grateful he gave Mylana a copy as a gift.*

Because he spoke Russian, he called me Les. Even though he couldn't relax his tongue enough to soften the *s*, I found it endearing, nonetheless. And much to my delight, he and Glenn got along really well.

He was also one of the most tormented people I've ever known, so even though it was shocking, it came as no surprise to me that he'd taken his own life. He'd left behind a loving fiancée and two daughters, a family, not to mention a worldwide community of friends and fans. He'd been a DJ at CJSR (the University of Alberta Radio Station) just like I had. In fact, that's where we met.

And now, he was gone. No more teatime. No more pool playing. No more on-air dedications. No more nihilism or brooding conversations. Just gone. I also realized that, although we'd driven through Edmonton on our way across Canada just a month earlier, I hadn't made it a point to visit him. I'd missed my chance.

Because we'd just moved, I wasn't in a position to go back to Edmonton for his "Celebration of Life." And because I wasn't close friends with his fiancée, I felt like I missed out on the opportunity to grieve with others. His sudden death and the profound sadness I was feeling with him being gone seemed to amplify the stress we were experiencing in our new life.

Only one or two Sundays later, after we'd gotten home from the Centre, I remember screaming and crying on the couch while Glenn sat beside me. I was so angry about how things were unfolding. I felt so disappointed in our life, in me, in Glenn not being able to find work. I was so tired of Mylana constantly asking when we were moving back to Toronto—*without even having given Victoria a chance.* I ranted and raved and at one point exclaimed (with my friend's suicide top of mind) that he'd had the right idea. "At least now *he* doesn't have to put up with any of this stupid life bullshit anymore!"

Then there was silence. And for once, Glenn didn't try to fix the situation or try to make me feel better. We sat quietly on the couch as I wept, feeling so monumentally defeated, useless, and utterly exhausted. Then, in a tender and quiet voice, he asked, "Love, what are you grateful for?"

I looked up at him and thought, maybe even said, "Nothing."

He asked again, "What are you grateful for? Just say anything…"

I don't remember what I said, but I know it was something simple like, "I'm grateful for the snot dripping down my face."

"What else?"

"I'm grateful I can breathe."

"What else?"

"I'm grateful I'm alive."

The more I expressed gratitude, the more I found things to be grateful for. Even though I didn't really feel grateful for anything at first, as I continued, I could feel myself starting to lighten up. After just a few minutes, I'd calmed down, and the tears had stopped. Glenn and I hugged, and we forged on with our day. Although there was a part of me that totally meant what I'd said about my friend having the right idea—that suicide was *an* answer—it wasn't *the* answer for me. I had created this experience that right now felt like a horrible mess, and I was determined to keep moving forward in creating the life I knew we were meant to live.

It would take a long time to get over my friend's death. When I think of him today, however, I think about not only the times we shared when we were younger, but also about the conversations I'd love to have with him now. I smile to myself knowing he'd have some strong opinions and even joke about the seriousness or validity of what I'm immersed in, but he'd be curious and open-minded enough to listen and support me, nonetheless.

* * *

A few weeks after we arrived in Victoria, I found work—as a clerk in a local health food and grocery store. It seemed twenty years' experience as an entrepreneur, business owner responsible for numerous staff and income streams, champion of sustainable practices, and advocate for "knowing who and where your food comes from" meant next to nothing.

Although I'd found a job, it felt like a long way down from where I'd been. I was making just above minimum wage and stocking grocery store shelves. After nearly twenty years of being in business for myself, I was embarrassed to be working retail. It also felt weird to take orders from people who were either just a few years older than my teenage daughter or who'd been doing their jobs for so long, it seemed like they weren't interested in doing things in different, perhaps better, ways.

A few weeks after starting work, however, I decided to "find the joy and value" in my work (something Rev. Jonathan had once said about how he approached bookkeeping), and soon realized that stocking cans of beans and soup and bags of cereal and pasta could actually be quite meditative. Knowing our home was still a bit of a shambles after the move—with some boxes yet to be unpacked and artwork still to be hung on the walls—these seemingly mindless, repetitive tasks at work became very calming. Where there was chaos at home, there was order at work.

In a couple of months, I managed to move my way up to supervisor, which meant more hours and more pay. I also met some amazing people, including two of my nearest and dearest West Coast friends (one of whom helped to edit this book).

* * *

The day I became friends with Janet, I was distraught. I was on the verge of tears because I'd just accidentally ripped the driver's side mirror off our car in the parkade. Not only was I upset because this meant a costly and unexpected repair, but I also knew Glenn had an out-of-town job interview the next day and needed the car to drive there. We didn't know if driving without a driver's-side mirror was a ticketable offense or not, not to mention the lack of visibility. We'd been in Victoria for a couple of months. Our money was running out. And now, not only did the car need to be repaired, but I also might have ruined Glenn's chances to get to his job interview.

As I was trying to work and think of what to do (and maintain some sense of composure), my co-worker, Janet, walked up to me. Very gently and compassionately, she asked me if I was okay. I told her "No," what had happened and how upset I was because Glenn had an interview the next day and no way of getting there. She looked at me and said, "Michael can drive him." I was dumbfounded. This lovely, kind woman and I had barely exchanged two words since I'd started working there (we worked in different departments, during different shifts) and here she was—she and her husband (whom we didn't even know)—ready to help us out.

Michael drove Glenn to that interview. Although nothing came of it, on the way there and back their friendship was forged, and our families have been friends ever since.

Making friends and building community was very slow going. It would take years before we even began to feel like we actually belonged in Victoria.

We'd moved from one part of the country to another, spoke the same language, and, on the surface, seemed to blend in. We also discovered that most of the people we met were from somewhere else, too. Yet there were many times we felt anywhere from mildly displaced to downright unwelcome. We were outsiders. No one cared who we were or what our life in Toronto had been all about.

They didn't care about our experience, what jobs we'd had, or how much money we'd made in our previous life.

Some native Victorians even found it offensive that we'd moved here at all, saying, "I wish people from Ontario would stop moving here. There's too much growth. We want to keep things the way they are."

It was unsettling. Even though we had just moved from one province to another within the same country, spoke the same language, and looked and sounded like pretty much everyone around us, we were strangers in a strange land, immigrants in our own country. It felt disheartening and bewildering, to say the least.

As the notion of not belonging crept in, we were hit with a crushing piece of news. The final payment for the last consulting job I'd done in Toronto wasn't coming through. The people who had taken over my business felt I hadn't lived up to my end of our arrangement and refused to pay the thousands of dollars owed. This payment was something we were counting on to get us through the next two to three months. And now we wouldn't be receiving it.

I was dumbfounded. I couldn't believe they felt I hadn't done the work agreed to. All those extra hours, all of that preparation. All of that guidance! Disbelief quickly turned to anger and anger to fear as I realized that without that money, we weren't going to be able to pay any of our bills or honour Mylana's school payment. We weren't going to be able to make the next car payment or pay the rent. Although I had already moved from part to full time at my job and had been promoted to supervisor of my department,

I was still working retail, bringing in less than half of what we needed to honour all of our financial commitments from month to month.

As hard as Glenn was trying, he wasn't working at all. Or rather he wasn't being paid for anything. It would take nearly a year of determination and perseverance, working with a counsellor at a local employment resource centre, sending out résumés daily, going to job fairs, weekly workshops, and several informational interviews before he would finally get a job. And when he did, it was a three-month remote contract for his old job back in Toronto.

We hadn't even been in Victoria for two months and already it felt like the dream we'd worked toward for two years was turning into a nightmare. Furthermore, not being able to honour our financial commitments began to stir up feelings of pain, anger, and fear as I began to view our current situation as a parallel to the financial failure of my bakery. The familiar voices saying, "You're not good enough," "You're not smart enough," and "You don't have what it takes" resurfaced with a vengeance.

As this financial reality sank in, I realized I'd have to tell our brand-new landlords—the ones who'd taken a leap of faith by renting to us—that we weren't in a position to pay our rent in full. It was humiliating, and I felt ashamed. Still, it had to be done.

The letter I wrote our landlords started off with gratitude because we felt so thankful to have landed in such a good place. I didn't go into the details of what had happened, just that circumstances were such that we were not in a position to pay our rent in full. I went on to say that we didn't want to make our problems their problems. The solution I offered was to pay our rent piecemeal, asking them if that might work. More gratitude, and then I sent the email.

The response I got back was filled with kindness, compassion, and pragmatism. As long as we could pay the rent within the month it was meant to be paid, that was fine. Their mortgage payments were directly dependent on us paying our rent on time. So as long as we could pay by the end of the month, that worked for them. Gratitude. Relief. But the rent was just one item on a long list requiring attention.

There were the school payments, car payments, my class tuition, utilities, groceries, and more. After a very gracious conversation with the school principal, I managed to secure a bursary for Mylana, which reduced our monthly payments. After a very heart-wrenching conversation with my aunt (who happened to be the co-signer on our car), she very generously agreed to temporarily take over the car payments. After conversations with my minister and teacher, I was able to barter health coaching for classes. And even after saying I didn't want to work in food anymore, I took on the odd baking gig for some extra income. An amazing bonus came in when we realized Glenn qualified for employment insurance because of the circumstances of our move—something we hadn't even considered.

It worked for a while and got us through October and November. However, as the weeks and months wore on, Glenn still wasn't working and we'd exhausted what little savings we had. We were broke. We could pay our rent, our proposal payment, and Mylana's tuition, but there was no money for anything else.

Now, I'm guessing that some of you reading this might be thinking, "Why didn't you just pull your daughter out of Montessori and save on private school fees?" Believe me, the thought crossed our minds, several times. However, parental guilt can be a strong motivator.

What I can tell you is that as excited as Glenn and I were to move, we were also very aware that we were taking Mylana away from the only life she'd ever known. Even though she was also looking forward to the move, I think there was a part of her that thought we wouldn't actually go through with it; that after a few months of this "experiment" we'd go back to Toronto, to her amazing life, and that would be that. But there was no "going back," and for Mylana, that was devastating. That devastation ended up being a pretty solid foundation for years of anger directed at us for having ripped her away from her idyllic life back East, including what she envisioned it would've been like had we stayed.

* * *

Mylana was born in our home, surrounded by a village. She grew up in a neighbourhood where there were no fences. Neighbouring kids played with each other, running across the backyards. Some of our neighbours even babysat Mylana from time to time. Her otherworldly friends (I'm purposely referring to them as "otherworldly" rather than "imaginary" because even though we couldn't see them, they were very real to her for years), Carson and Mr. Yaya, lived on our street.

One winter evening, when Mylana was about two and a half, she announced she was going to visit Carson and Yaya. She began to put on her little red snowsuit and boots as my visiting mom

101

looked on in bewilderment. When she couldn't quite grasp the door handle to open the door, I helped. As Mylana walked outside on her own, my mom asked defiantly, "Lesiu, aren't you going to stop her?" To which I replied, "No." I poked my head out the door and ended up joining her just before she crossed the street.

I watched her as she went up to ring the doorbell to Carson and Yaya's house (the house of neighbours who'd recently moved in). When no one answered the door, we crossed back to our side of the street and walked back home. Mylana had had her adventure, I'd allowed my daughter the space to follow her imagination, and my mom had nearly had a heart attack. But all was fine. When we moved out West, I wanted to keep things as fine for Mylana as they could be. Continuing with Montessori seemed the best way to do so.

Mylana started Montessori at the age of three, and it was an extraordinary fit—for her and for us. We were even told by her very first Casa teacher, just a few weeks into her first year, that Mylana was "the quintessential Montessori student."

Until she graduated grade six, Mylana spent most of her time at school. She was there five days a week during the school year and at spring and summer camps in between. She was there for before care and after care throughout most of the year. Her best friends went to that school and many of her friends' parents eventually became our friends, too. And because I spent several years of Mylana's early life focusing on my bakery, Mylana spent more time with her teachers and care providers than she did with her own mom.

When it came time to consider what school Mylana would attend when we got to the West Coast, we decided that continuing with Montessori was the best thing for all of us. Aside from living with her parents, it would be the one thing to anchor her in the otherwise total upheaval of life as she'd known it.

So yes, we could've sent her to public school and had an additional thousand dollars per month or more. To us, however, the value of Mylana continuing with Montessori outweighed the value of what that additional money could've paid for. In addition to the exceptional education we knew she'd receive, Montessori was the foundation of continuity we felt our daughter needed to thrive, and it was non-negotiable.

We'd done all we could think of, cut our expenses in every way we could muster, yet it wasn't enough. If something didn't change, in my mind, we were going to end up on the street or living out of our car. As the anxiety, shame, and guilt expanded, the more I began to spiral into panic.

Even in that state of panic, though, I found myself trying to be creative. I still had a gym membership and could shower there. Maybe Glenn and I could live out of the car and Mylana could live at her new best friend's house (at least she'd live under a roof with a family and someone she went to school with). By living in our car, we'd save on rent, be able to get back on our feet, and within a few months find another place to live. We even talked about this desperate-sounding option to our very new friends.

To their credit and our relief, they didn't bat an eye, and said, "Yes, absolutely," that Mylana could come and live with them. They could empathize. They'd moved here from Ottawa at the same time we'd moved from Toronto and were experiencing trials and tribulations of their own. It seemed for all of us, the reality hadn't yet caught up to the dream.

Eventually, one Sunday I spoke with our minister, Rev. Carrie. She listened with an open heart and with so much kindness and compassion. After doing a Spiritual Mind Treatment, she said, "Lesia, why don't you and your family do a crowdfunding campaign?" I was shocked. What? Was she serious? Crowdfunding? No way.

"You're struggling, and it's so hard to thrive when you're barely surviving." She told me she was sure that if I reached out to the community and asked for support, people would jump at the chance to help us.

I couldn't even fathom it. No one had died. No one needed emergency surgery. And even though the option loomed in my mind, we weren't homeless. Forget it. There was no way. Asking people for money was *not* an option.

So for another month (which felt like a decade), we kept on scrimping and barely making it. But somehow, make it we did.

As our first Christmas on the West Coast drew nearer, the weather got colder—way colder, with tonnes of actual snow— which was not supposed to happen here. I missed my friends and continued being hit by waves of sustained grief over the sudden suicide of my dear friend. I thought back to something Rev. Carrie had said: "If you don't ask your friends and community for help, you're taking away their opportunity to give, to support you."

The more I thought about it, the more something in me stirred. I let Glenn know I thought we should do what Rev. Carrie suggested and ask our community for help.

It would take everything I had to wade through the guilt and shame I was feeling, to become so vulnerable in front of pretty much everyone we knew. It would take another ginormous leap of faith to let folks know that—after we'd made such a big deal out of moving here—things weren't working out and that we could really do with their support. It would take all the tenacity, fortitude, and gumption I could muster to move forward with this new plan.

Glenn still wasn't convinced but agreed to go along with it. I sat down, and over the next couple of days, wrote the crowdfunding letter, taking great care to be honest, factual, and as gracious as I could be, knowing I was about to air what felt like the dirtiest of laundry.

* * *

Dear friends and family,
Firstly, thank you for your friendship, love, and support—today and always…!

Secondly, thank you for taking the time to read this.

*It is taking a lot of courage to write this letter because **no one is sick, no one is dying, no one is homeless**. We live in a first world country, have a roof over our heads, Mylana goes to school, and we have clothes on our backs. And for all of this, we are so thankful…!*

As I write I feel ashamed, I feel embarrassed, I feel I'm a fraud, and sometimes I feel like we've made the biggest mistake of our lives by leaving Toronto, and coming to Victoria…

Because of the challenges we've faced since coming to Victoria, we've neglected most of our friends back east because of not wanting to answer the #1 question asked, "How's it going... ?"

Sadly, it's been easier to not stay in touch, rather than feel like we need to lie about how great it's been since we moved here, not wanting to give any more energy to the challenges we've faced by even talking about them. But this also means, for many of you, we haven't kept in touch, and for that, we're truly sorry. We hope you can forgive us, while we forgive ourselves.

Now, with great humility and some apprehension, we open ourselves up to our friends, and are asking for your help to get through the next couple of months as we find our way with our new life...

As many of you know, 2 years ago, while on our first bona fide family vacation in Victoria, Glenn, Mylana and I fell in love with this beautiful place and the amazing energy here, and immediately answered an incredibly strong pull/call to move here.

After lots of dreaming, planning, purging, and tearful goodbyes with friends, family, community, and business, we packed up what was left of our Toronto life in our car, and headed west for a 10-day journey across our gorgeous, expansive country which eventually landed us in our new west coast home. What an incredible experience!

Since arriving in Victoria 4 months ago we have been blessed with so much:

- *We rent a unit in a lovely house, with amazing downstairs neighbours.*
- *We have awesome, attentive landlords.*

- *Our home is a 2-minute walk away from Mylana's new school; and although Mylana misses her friends in Toronto sooooo much (and is ready to move back at the drop of a hat), she has made some friends here, and has adapted well to her new school (thank you Kew Park for an amazing foundation!!!); she's a trouper!*

- *I got a part-time job as a grocery clerk the first week we got here, which became full-time after a few weeks, and led to a promotion as supervisor of the department a couple of months later; although this is a low-paying job, and far from my ideal line of work, it allows us to pay many of our bills, affords us a discount on groceries and household items, and has given me the opportunity to interact with new people every day.*

- *We stepped into and were immediately embraced by the Centre for Spiritual Living Victoria community, and remain very active as members and volunteers; this community has been our main source of support since moving here, and we are forever grateful for the kindness, generosity and love we've been, and continue to be shown.*

- *We've gone from zero income when we moved here, to bringing in about 75% of what we need for our expenses as of this moment— huzzah!*

- *After constant searching, several interviews, what seems like never-ending testing, engaging in workshops, and attending a weekly group at our local WorkBC office, we know Glenn is one day closer to connecting with his perfect job; because Glenn is currently unemployed, we get gas vouchers from this community office, which afford us about 1/3 of the gas we use for the month.*

- *Thanks to the generosity of CSL Victoria, I had the opportunity to attend the Circle of Love Gathering up island in October—a mind-blowing, heart-opening, consciousness-expanding event which reaffirmed for me my family and I are on the right path towards our highest good, and Victoria is where we are meant to be right now.*

For all of the above—we are so thankful!

However... our savings are now used up. We recently borrowed money from family who have been in a position to help, and although things are improving and we are moving forward every day, we are currently unable to honour our financial commitments in full, on time— including rent. We are now in a position where we are unable to afford groceries.

We are all healthy. We have a home. Mylana goes to school. And we are grateful.

We know we are valued members of our new, growing community here, and are so very, very grateful for the support we continue to receive from the CSL Victoria community, and the new friends we are making here.

We know the Universe always has our backs, and we are supported physically, emotionally, spiritually, and financially—even when it doesn't look or feel like it.

We are also forever grateful to our CSL Toronto community—our friends, my path to Spiritual Practitioner Studies and Ministerial Studies, and for giving us the tools to do the mental, spiritual, and emotional work we do every day to keep our faith strong—faith in us, faith in our belief we made the right choice in starting a new chapter of our lives in Victoria, and faith in Spirit always having our backs— NO MATTER WHAT!

So, knowing everyone has their own needs and challenges, we very humbly ask, and would be so very, very, very grateful for your help to get us through the next few months.

If you are in a position to help with a donation—thank you…!

If you are in a position to help us with work and community connections in Victoria—thank you…!

And for those of you who are able and willing, we welcome all affirmative prayers, visions, and holding of our family as perfect, whole, and complete in your consciousness—thank you…!

Thank you, thank you, thank you…!!!

And finally, with enormous gratitude, I feel some relief in being able to finally face that #1 question we've been avoiding for so long, knowing we are safe, we are loved, and we've finally been able to give an honest answer to our friends, and to open ourselves up to you, by asking for help.

We love you and miss you all—a lot…

With so much love and gratitude,
Lesia (and Glenn and Mylana)

And then, with similar trepidation and anticipation I felt four years earlier when sending my email about the closing of LPK's, I hit *enter*.

What happened next felt nothing short of miraculous.

Within minutes, donation after donation started pouring in—from friends, family, community members, past clients of mine—from people we had *just* met! Day after day after day, the gifts of what I can only call pure love and loving kindness just continued to flow. And even though money was definitely what we needed to pay our bills and buy groceries, the love and compassion that came our way was nothing short of extraordinary.

I had been on the giving end plenty of times before and knew how amazing, empowering, and life-affirming it can feel to give. To be on the receiving end of that givingness, though, was an entirely different kind of experience.

Every time we read an accompanying response from someone, we could feel the love and compassion in our bodies, growing, expanding, and exploding with each donation, with each confirmation. I don't know why it took me so by surprise, but I just couldn't believe that so many people actually cared so much about us. Truth be told, I could believe they cared that much about Glenn and Mylana. I had a hard time believing, however, they actually cared that much about *me*.

Thanks to the ongoing generosity of our friends, family, and community, we surpassed our goal and received enough money to get through the next two months. We were able to buy groceries, pay our rent, and all of our bills—on time and in full. We were also able to get a Christmas tree and to have a small but celebratory Christmas dinner with our new friends and chosen Victoria family.

Most of all, though, being on the receiving end of such an extraordinary amount of love, compassion, and givingness shifted something in me and in us as a family. It reignited that rock-solid knowing that in spite of all the challenges we had endured since leaving Toronto, regardless of what was waiting for us two months down the road, paraphrasing my fellow classmate Rev. Eric Overholtzer, we were right where we were meant to be, and we were meant to be right where we were. We were experiencing exactly what was ours to experience.

No matter how much Mylana asked, even implored, "When are we going back home to Toronto?" and no matter how many times some of our Toronto friends would say, "You'll be back," Glenn and I both knew, *there was no going back.*

Section 2

Unearthing and Exploring
(Beliefs)

Chapter 4

Awareness

"You cannot set bone until you know where it is broken, and you cannot set upon the journey of individuation—of becoming a whole person—until you know where and how you are divided."

– Mark Nepo, *Seven Thousand Ways to Listen*

In the first section of this book, I shared three main stories that have been integral to my life experience so far. I talked about my tenuous relationship with my dad and the financial failure and subsequent fallout of closing my bakery. I also shared how, at various times during our cross-country move, I wondered whether or not we'd made a colossal mistake in uprooting our family from our solid life in Toronto to begin a new life on the West Coast.

The first two stories illustrate how living in fear and feeling like an epic failure for most of my life seemed to cause, even fuel, situations that further perpetuated the pain, anger, and fear that had been the foundation from which I'd lived my life thus far. For most of my life, I wasn't even aware this was going on. Without knowing it, those feelings had become so deeply ingrained, I had accepted—very early on life—that to live in a constant state of fear and feel like a failure was normal. Because I wasn't even aware this was happening or why, for decades, I lived life on autopilot, with three main beliefs driving the proverbial bus and plotting the course for further experiences rooted in more pain, more anger, and more fear.

A key element of Soul Excavation is becoming aware of the limiting thoughts, stories, and beliefs that have kept us feeling stuck. Awareness is knowledge, recognition, or grasp of something. Without awareness, it can feel almost impossible to move forward in life in a new or different way.

When I sat down to write this chapter, I must've written out about forty limiting beliefs, all having to do with the stories of the first three chapters. The more I looked at them, though, the more I realized that, even if they sounded different, when reduced to their essence, really, only three main beliefs came into play:

- "You're not good enough."
- "You're not smart enough."
- "You don't have what it takes."

Although these beliefs, cautions, or however they were intended, were originally offered by my dad, the voice that kept repeating them for decades was my own.

By the Leap of Faith chapter, I had spent nearly every Sunday in the four months preceding our departure at CSL Toronto inspired by Rev. Jonathan and the Science of Mind teachings. This new world of mysticism and metaphysics had such a profound effect on me that a few weeks before heading out West, I stepped into my first class and deliberate foray into spiritual/consciousness studies. It was during the course of that ten-week class—the first one I attended online after arriving in Victoria—that I experienced the profoundly compelling, activational call to ministry.

As I delved further into the Science of Mind philosophy, not only did I become aware of the limiting beliefs that had been in play for most of my life, I also came to realize the profound impact of accepting these three main limiting beliefs—knowingly or otherwise. I came to realize these beliefs just weren't true. Those beliefs were just ideas I'd held onto for a long, long time. They weren't Who and What I am at my core.

It would take several years to work through those beliefs. Letting go of them wasn't easy.

For years, I'd work through one belief, just to discover there was another buried deeper beneath it. As I dug into that one, the original would rear its ugly head once again. Even as I began to entertain a new, more expansive view of the world and what was possible, the old beliefs would resurface again and again.

I played tug-of-war with them and they with me, causing me to feel caught in a "three steps forward and two steps back" progression as we prepared for and eventually moved from Toronto to Victoria. The more I explored, however, the more empowered I felt. For the first time in my life, I was actually getting to the underlying cause of why I viewed myself and the world the way I did. *Finally*, by becoming aware of the limiting beliefs that had been in play for so much of my life, I was able to do something about them!

So what was the deal? Why did I cling so tightly and reverently to these thoughts, beliefs, and feelings that kept me so firmly rooted in pain, anger, and fear? Why couldn't I just let go of them and turn to new beliefs that were more life-affirming—ones that made me feel good enough, smart enough, and that I have what it takes?

* * *

For as long as I can remember, memories of my childhood have been patchy. Memories of young adulthood—same thing. The former because of compartmentalizing and dissociating—common ways of coping with intense fear and significant, ongoing trauma and abuse. The latter, due mainly to abuse of alcohol and recreational drugs as a way of coping with the former.

In my early twenties, I met and worked with a counsellor at the Addiction Research Foundation. Even though I wasn't entirely convinced I was an alcoholic, I was willing to work with her. It was during our very first conversation, I realized—what friends had been telling me for some time—that I did indeed have an addictive, abusive relationship with alcohol.

So what if I drank and partied like most of my friends? Wasn't social drinking normal? Sure. So what if I let off steam on the weekend and perhaps a few days during the week by going out and getting drunk? Didn't everyone? Not necessarily. Okay, well, didn't everyone black out after a few beers, still appearing functional to those around them, even to the point of being able to drive home (and not remembering having done so)? Um, no—*not by a long shot.*

After only a few sessions with this lovely, frank, and supportive woman, I began to realize that my reasons for drinking went way beyond partying with friends. It wasn't normal for people to black out and not remember entire chunks of their lives due to overconsumption of alcohol. Being able to drink most of my guy friends under the table wasn't actually noteworthy. Going to work half-drunk, after waking up in a bed soaked with my own urine, still reeking of alcohol from the night before was not only not functional, but it was also disrespectful to those around me. The only one I was fooling was myself.

Why am I sharing this? Because it took working with this counsellor and giving up alcohol to realize that most of the choices I'd made through my teens and early-adult life were founded in beliefs rooted in fear, pain, and zero self-esteem. Additionally, the choices I'd made while drunk and high were even more messed up because there was no way I could think clearly or rationally in an inebriated state.

There's a solid argument for not allowing even the most *minute* amount of alcohol in the blood when driving. *Alcohol changes the chemistry and operability of the brain.* And, if the brain—the tool with which we use our minds, our imagination, and how we express that Infinite, Universal Energy we innately are—isn't working properly, then it only stands to reason that for most of us, we'll likely end up making even poorer choices while inebriated. Whatever beliefs were in play for me when sober, often became mega-amplified while I was high and drunk, causing me to make even more destructive choices under the guise of feeling uninhibited and free.

Looking back now, being labelled an alcoholic by that student psychiatrist probably saved my life. In order to really begin the exploration of what was keeping me stuck in a swirling miasma of fear, pain, anger, and despair, first I had to get present for the excavation. There was no way that could possibly happen if I was constantly self-medicating.

On December 1, 1992, I finally stopped drinking. In a matter of days, the pain, anger, and fear I thought I had been feeling my entire life exploded to the surface. As it did, I realized that I hadn't felt much of anything for years. Instead, I'd been numbing and suppressing. Once those feelings started to surface, finally having to face them head-on felt nothing short of terrifying.

For years, there were tears, confusion, and so much anger. There was also no shortage of impatience. My therapist would analyze and offer nuggets of wisdom and I'd expect to get better "just like that." For a long time, I thought if I could just bring everything to light and dissect it all, I could think my way to feeling unbroken, to feeling whole. And over time, it worked—to a degree.

Now here's the thing: Even though I'd spent all of that time, energy, and attention on working through emotions and history, it really wasn't until the intensive two-year Spiritual Practitioner Studies program with Dr. James Mellon, that I really began to dig, in earnest, through the layers upon layers of beliefs that had kept me feeling stuck for so long.

The intensive two-year program accredited through the Emerson Theological Institute and the Holmes Institute for Consciousness Studies was and continues to be one of the deepest, richest, and most profound experiences of my life so far. During this two-year journey, I was able to *finally* become aware of *why*—for most of my life—I'd felt like I could only become "so" successful, or make "so" much money, or feel "so" happy, but not be able to move beyond that.

As we dug into how life got to be the way it was, we explored things like family history, sexuality, world religions, values, and—you guessed it—beliefs. The more my fellow classmates and I looked into our beliefs and the impact they have on our life experience, the more aware I became of why those three main stories of my life had unfolded the way they had. I began to understand why my relationship with my dad had been so tenuous, why my bakery had seemingly failed, and why—even as I questioned moving out West—I was already aware of something in me that knew there was no going back and that we were headed exactly where we were meant to be.

With this new awareness, I was able to understand something that changed my way of looking at the world from that point onward.

I am not my thoughts, feelings, or experiences. *I am not my beliefs.*

Chapter 5

Understanding

"Identity is felt as one's soul finding its weight and measure. We know who we are because we have uncovered the stuff of which we are made."

- Thomas Moore, *Care of the Soul*

I originally went into Spiritual Practitioner Studies because the program was a mandatory stepping stone toward ministerial studies. What came as a surprise, however, was that only two or three weeks into the program, I quickly realized this leg of my spiritual journey was not just a stepping stone to what I thought was my ultimate goal. Practitioner studies were just as much part of my journey as anything that had come before and anything that would come after.

From day one, the pace was unrelenting, with no time to pause or marinate on anything. It was very much "show up, do the work, or get left behind." In addition to our weekly class, the days and nights in between were filled with at least ten hours of rigorous homework.

Right from the start, I felt like I was playing catch-up. Still, there was no way I was getting left behind. I was "all in." Not only was this a significant investment of time and money, I was also determined to succeed so I could move forward with my plans to become a New Thought minister.

Every week, we read from at least three different books, poring through modules, preparing salient points for class discussion, and writing thought papers. I'd arrive online for our weekly class—with a pit in my stomach, heightened by intermittent waves of nausea—as we waited, knowing that, at some point, Dr. James would call on each of us to "stand and deliver," expecting us to explain a section of his choosing from any of the three books or source material we'd worked through the previous week. We were also learning how to perform Spiritual Mind Treatment— the key transformational, activational technique that determines the effectiveness and success of a spiritual practitioner.

At the end of every semester, there was an essay, a detailed report about the paid spiritual practitioner session we were required to have, and a comprehensive three-hour exam. If you didn't pass, you didn't move on.

Consistently, we were challenged to dig and keep digging—to explore old stories and limiting beliefs, and to face beliefs head-on that may have been gnawing away at us for the better part of our lives. During this process, we'd invariably unearth and discover beliefs we hadn't even known were there. That messy, exhaustive exploration continued, often to the point of my brain actually hurting because the expansion was causing physical changes in my body and body chemistry. Just when I thought I'd unearthed the bulk of the pain, anger, and fear that had been my foundation for so long, I'd discover that wait—*there's more.*

During the second year, we moved into the practical application of what we'd studied and explored in year one. Ready to push the boundaries of self-discovery, self-reliance, and the value and accessibility of practitioner work even further, Dr. James threw the decade-old syllabus out the window and created the program anew—as we were going through it!

At the end of year two, we also had our oral panels. Only those who'd passed the written final could move on to the orals. On top of all of that, throughout our two-year journey there were numerous personal challenges and milestones that impacted our collective, including death, divorce, relocation, marriage, career change, and the beginning of the global Covid-19 experience. We started the program with fifteen. Seven graduated.

During those two years, it felt like one day I'd be digging through topsoil, easily unearthing and revealing little nuggets of wisdom and gems of brilliance along the way—shining a light on the nuances, choices, habits, and tendencies regarding family, health, money, and career that had made up my life so far. Then I'd hit clay, and the digging would get harder. Then, just as I'd gotten used to digging through clay with a new set of tools and a deeper sense of resolve, I'd hit a layer of sand that seemed to keep falling back in on itself, making it that much more challenging to excavate the beliefs I was so desperately trying to reveal. After finally making it through the sand, I'd hit shale and would diligently chip away at it, coming to know that at some point, another nugget or gem would eventually be unearthed. I was determined to keep digging, knowing that at the bottom of this excavation was the *real* me—the me that had been buried under a lifetime of pain, anger, and fear.

What was so incredible, however, was that it wasn't only about digging to the bottom to find the real me. It was also about everything that was discovered and revealed along the way. It was about having to navigate the different layers of awareness, using different tools to work through each of those layers. It was about discovering the various insights and wisdom and the compassion and forgiveness that revealed themselves along the way—for myself, and surprisingly, for my dad.

Sometimes it was easy, but more often it felt hard. It was dirty, gritty, laborious work that often had me in tears and left me feeling completely raw, vulnerable, and gross—like I couldn't stand to be in my own skin. All I wanted to do was stop, take a break, even crawl into bed and just go to sleep. Ultimately, however, the journey itself—one of epic understanding—was just as much the treasure as was rediscovering the real me that had been buried under years and layers of crap.

This ongoing exploration—the digging and unearthing and discovery—is what I came to call *Soul Excavation*. Because the further I dug, the more I was able to unearth and explore. And the more I explored, the more I was able to dig through so much of the muck that I'd been buried under—or more accurately, that I'd been holding onto—for most of my life.

Not only holding onto, but actually *identifying as.* Somewhere along the line, I had become my pain, anger, and fear. I had decided—I don't know when—that I wasn't good enough, I wasn't smart enough, and I didn't have what it took to live a successful, fulfilling, joyful life. Even with all that, however, because I had already been immersed in spiritual/consciousness studies for two years leading up to this program, there was something in me that kept persevering as we faced our challenges leading up to and after our move across country, and there was something in me that was no longer satisfied with how life had been up until now.

In the Science of Mind philosophy, there are three main things we teach:

- **There is only one thing going on.** Call it God, the Universe, Energy, Love, or the quantum field—whatever is meaningful for you. It is the very essence of everyone and everything. It is infinite in scope (boundless, limitless, eternal) and creative by nature (it's always shifting, changing, evolving, and expanding).
- **Everyone and everything is that one thing.** In other words, we are all walking, talking, living, breathing, unique, original expressions of Infinite Creative Energy. This includes tangible things like people, places, and things. It also includes intangible things like thoughts, beliefs, and feelings. God is all there is. Energy is all there is. There is nothing that isn't God. There is nothing that isn't Energy.
- **We live according to spiritual and natural laws, with the main law being the law of cause and effect.** From a scientific perspective, you kick a ball, it moves. You kick a wall, and either the wall is dented, or your foot breaks. From a spiritual perspective, what you think, believe, and feel becomes the foundation for your life experience.

One of the aspects of God/Energy/Love is the realm where all beliefs and all memories of all time reside. The beliefs we focus on—knowingly or unknowingly—are the ones that end up having the biggest impact on our life experience. What we focus on expands, or as Dr. Joe Dispenza would say, "Where you put your attention, is where you put your energy." Think you're not worthy and deserving of happiness? Guess what, you'll end up finding evidence in your life time and time again to prove that hypothesis—that belief—until you choose to believe something different.

We can also look at it from a quantum perspective. No matter what your worldview, let's just go on a little journey together. If, as has been shown through quantum physics, you allow yourself to accept that at its most foundational, elemental level, everything is energy, it would only stand to reason that everyone and everything is energy—including you and me. Because energy is infinite in scope (boundless, limitless, eternal), creative by nature (always shifting, changing, evolving, and expanding), then *so are we*. Because the quantum field—the realm where everything is possible—isn't bound by time and space (i.e., you don't have to wait or travel to another location to experience anything)—then *everything* is possible, right here, right now.

If there is only energy, and nothing else, then we—as energy that is infinite in scope and creative by nature—are all interconnected. As energy, we are not bound by time and space (even though it may seem like it in a world filled with clocks and schedules, maps, and GPS). We are simultaneously interconnected *to* and *as* our past, present, and future—all at the same time, everywhere all at once.

Understanding

So, if we—as interconnected expressions of energy that are infinite in scope and creative by nature—are interconnected with our past, present, and future right here, right now, does it not stand to reason that all beliefs of all time would be available and accessible at all times? If yes, would it not also mean that most of the beliefs we've been believing—knowingly or unknowingly— are indeed not even ours to begin with?

When we become aware that there are infinite beliefs just hangin' out in a sea of infinite possibilities, we can begin to cut ourselves some slack. We can begin to realize that some of our longstanding beliefs are part of our familial history, our culture, the society we live in, media, institutions, politics, and the collective and race consciousness, and so much more. It's no wonder, then, that the energetic pull of what so many around us think and believe can feel so strong. It's no wonder it can feel so hard to think and believe something different or new.

However, because we are all unique, original expressions of God/ Energy/Love—or the quantum field—we are always at choice as to how much of our "true selves" we allow to show up or express. It even goes beyond being at choice—we are constantly *choosing*. As we put our attention—consciously or unconsciously—on a wave of infinite possibility in the quantum field, that possibility instantaneously becomes an actualized part(icle) that we experience in/as our life. This is a very simple way of illustrating that "thoughts are things."

Want a different life experience? Choose to think and believe something new. Better yet, choose to think and believe something new mindfully, with intention, on purpose. Why leave it up to chance, when you can actually direct your energy by placing your attention on something you actually desire? Why not start creating your life by design, rather than by default?

When I first started to wrap my head around the idea that I am always at choice—even when it might seem like there is no choice to be made—it was incredibly empowering. I learned that, after years of living according to someone else's beliefs and expectations, in this present moment, I could choose something different. Based on that choice, I could create a new life experience. *Mind blown.*

As simple as this concept is, though, it's not necessarily easy to embrace and can be even more challenging to embody. For me, I was totally hooked on the idea of creating my new life based on thinking new thoughts and embracing new beliefs. I knew, however, that I needed to dig into and unearth exactly what beliefs I'd been holding onto first—especially those I wasn't even aware of—before I could really experience any lasting change in my life. I had to understand what those beliefs were before I could shift my attention to new beliefs that allowed me to feel confident and powerful, and that life was filled with infinite possibilities.

Understanding is another key element of Soul Excavation. It is the comprehension, digestion, or assimilation of something. It's a deepened awareness that allows us to make sense of or further examine something that has recently come to light. As I became crystal clear on the limiting beliefs that had been in play for so much of my life, I was also able to understand the impact they'd had and would continue to have unless I let them go.

Even with the various tools and support I'd had throughout my life, it took a long time to let go of the three main beliefs that had kept me living from pain, anger, and fear for most of my life. It wasn't until I truly began to understand how deeply rooted they were, I could finally begin to do something about them.

So how can we do it? How can we shift from identifying as the pain, anger, and fear we've experienced for so long to embracing the confidence, power, and infinite possibilities that allow us to live the abundant, prosperous, fulfilling life we want—the life we are fully capable of living?

My absolute favourite, #1 tool to get me or my client from feeling stuck in the muck to feeling liberated, powerful, and whole, is Spiritual Mind Treatment.

* * *

An activational technique, also known as Affirmative Prayer, Spiritual Mind Treatment (Treatment for short) argues for the truth beyond immediate circumstances—*no matter what is going on.* It is the main tool used by spiritual practitioners to consciously, intentionally move energy (or shift the practitioner's mindset) for a specific purpose. It is performed using words or in silence, with the practitioner going through a series of steps that include:

- **Recognizing** there is only God/Energy/Love.
- **Identifying** with every fibre of one's being *as* God/Energy/ Love and knowing the same for everyone and everything (including our client).

- **Declaring** or **realizing** the specific intention of the Treatment/Prayer. It is all done in the present tense, using only positive, affirmative language (we don't bring the problem into the Treatment). There is no wishing or hoping here. We are knowing the truth and infinite potentiality of the situation. We are tapping into and drawing from the completed vision of our intention.

- Expressing **gratitude**, knowing the Treatment/Prayer is already a successful done deal and that our intention is fully realized and fully orbed—right here, right now.

- **Releasing** any attachment to outcome, knowing that God/Energy/Love is doing its thing, working its magic, and taking care of the *how* now that we've been clear on the *what* of our intention. This is about trust, faith, and moving forward in life from a new, higher level of Consciousness or awareness and acceptance (a more positive, life-affirming mindset), rather than going back to focusing on the problem and constantly wondering, "Is it done yet?"

In order for Spiritual Mind Treatment to be effective, however, it is absolutely critical to get clear on our beliefs. Or rather, it's critical to get clear on any limiting beliefs that may still be in play. For whatever beliefs are in play, the spirit or energy or vibration of those beliefs will be what powers our prayer.

* * *

Awareness and understanding, two key aspects of Soul Excavation, can look and feel different from person to person, from moment to moment. Whether it's working with a spiritual practitioner or coach, getting out into nature, writing in a journal, listening to music, reading self-empowerment books, moving your body, taking classes, learning something new, creating art, or meditating quietly, there's no one way that works for everyone. The key is being willing enough to get messy—to dig, unearth, and explore—however it works for you.

As we expand our awareness and deepen our understanding, we come to realize—with every fibre of our being—that ultimately, Who we are, "the stuff of which we are made" is infinitely more powerful, creative, and resilient than anything we could ever think, believe, or feel; than *anything* we could ever experience.

Chapter 6

Realization

"Finding our soul has to do with becoming conscious of our true identity and discovering our purpose for living."
        – Paul Levy, *The Quantum Revelation*

"Who do you think you are?"

This is a question many of us have heard at some point in our lives. Most of the time—at least in my experience—with the emphasis being on the word "who," the question comes across as more of an insinuation, as if to point out perhaps I've bitten off more than I can chew, or that I'm reaching beyond my grasp. Often, it can even sound like an accusation, which I now know really has more to do with the person asking the question, rather than the person being asked.

One of my favourite variations of this question is a version brought to life by Kevin, a co-worker and friend Glenn and I used to work with many, *many* years ago. "Who do you think you are … *anyways?*" was just one of many hilarious catchphrases casually thrown into conversation by this vibrant, charismatic, and exuberantly entertaining man.

An artist, dancer, and actor, Kevin always delivered this line with such flamboyance and flair, with just the right amount of pause after the word "are," and just enough emphasis on the word "anyways," making everyone within earshot burst into laughter. Decades later, Kevin's spin on this question still has Glenn and me chuckling anytime one of us brings it up.

A few years ago, while preparing for a Sunday guest talk on "Imagination" for Unity Victoria (now Unity Vancouver Island), I realized that this question (which was initially born of melodrama and hyperbole) was actually a great activational prompt when it came to considering how we use our imaginations—especially when it comes to creating our life experience. As a result, it became the focal point and title of that talk.

As I prepared for my talk, it occurred to me that every word in that question had value, and as soon as the emphasis or focus changed, so did the nuanced meaning of the question.

In shifting the focus from "who" to "you," the question can come across as more of an indication or even criticism that you're trying to be something other than what someone else expects you to be. Even though it may seem like an invitation to the person being asked to contemplate and evaluate whether or not they're heading in the right direction, once again, it still has more to do with the person doing the asking (along with their own expectations), rather than the person being asked.

When moving on to the word "think," I find it gets even more interesting. If, as so many New Thought teachers and thinkers and quantum physicists espouse, "thoughts are things," then what we think becomes our life experience. As such, it doesn't matter what anyone else says, thinks, or expects of us. Our thoughts create *our* reality, period. However, if we believe (knowingly or unknowingly) that what others think does matter, then we'll likely be looking for validation from others, or will constantly be second-guessing ourselves because we think we don't know how to trust our own gut or intuition.

As we move on to the word "are," we enter the realm of action and activation (the igniting spark that impels us into taking action). There's a commonly used phrase in the Science of Mind teaching philosophy by Ernest Holmes, "Treat and move your feet." It means that it's one thing to think, contemplate, or envision, but without actually stepping into action, what you're really doing is passive dreaming. You're simply wishing and hoping and are likely to get more of what you've experienced up until now. If, however, after letting the Universe know you're serious about your dream, you actually do something—no matter how small—that is in keeping with your true identity, you actually open up yourself to the opportunity of experiencing something different or new.

And then, there's Kevin's irreverent addition of the pause and emphasis on "anyways." Even though I'm sure Kevin wasn't thinking about the nuanced meaning of this variation on a theme way back when he came up with it, the more I thought about it, the more I realized that *this* is the most important part of the question. Why? Because "anyway" (which is the correct version of the commonly misused "anyways") is a synonym for "regardless."

137

In exchanging "anyways" with "regardless," the question becomes, "Who do you think you are...*regardless*?" I see this as a reminder that regardless of whatever I am thinking, feeling, or experiencing, there is something else behind those thoughts, feelings, and experiences. For me, that "something" is the thing that begs exploration.

Kevin's version of this question is an open invitation to dig beyond the beliefs that have been the lens through which we've viewed the world and ourselves so far. It's an opportunity to look beyond where we've been choosing to put our attention up until now.

It's a prompt to become aware of and understand that our perceptions shape our life experience. Furthermore, it opens the door to realizing (a deepened understanding that inspires us into action that is another key element of Soul Excavation): That—regardless of what anyone says, thinks, or expects—we are always choosing and creating our life experience based on those choices.

As this realization expands, the more empowered and inspired we become to intentionally and purposefully shift from identifying with longstanding limiting beliefs that have kept us feeling stuck in pain, anger, fear, anxiety, overwhelm, confusion, and with low self-esteem. The more activated we become, the more we begin embracing new, more positive, life-affirming beliefs that empower us to recognize our worth and what we are capable of. When we discover our self-worth, we begin to see and cultivate the value in everyone and everything in our life.

We discover, expect, and attract more respect, compassion, and love in our relationships. We muster the confidence to ask for a raise at work. We have more patience with and time for our kids. We open a new business, write our first book, finally make ourselves a priority, and dare to live our dreams. We listen more and talk less. We accept more and judge less. We try more and procrastinate less. We love more and worry less. We do all of this, *regardless* of who we think we have been until now because we finally know that we are infinitely more powerful, creative, and resilient than anything we could ever think, believe, or feel—than *anything* we could ever experience.

* * *

In June of 2020, inspired by years of thought-provoking, mind-blowing, and consciousness-expanding after-dinner conversations on the couch with Glenn and some of our friends, Glenn and I started a podcast. After much consideration of what to call our show—an exploration of how our thoughts, feelings, and beliefs create our reality—we decided upon, "Who Do You Think You Are?"

After weeks of practice, the intention for our first episode was to have an organic, engaging, conscious conversation about whatever bubbled up. Immediately after introducing our guest, Rev. Kelly Bershinsky, I spontaneously asked him, "Rev. Kelly, who do you think you are?" To which he replied. "Well, if I only knew that I probably wouldn't be on this podcast." In that very moment, the anchoring component of our show, and the impetus for every subsequent conversation, was born.

It took a few years to get to that first episode, and much of that had to do with the beliefs that were floating around in the background (even front and centre) as I wondered if it was really a good idea, if we had what it took to put on a good show, and, once we unleashed it into the world, would anyone actually care and listen to what we had to say. I now know that the three main beliefs that had been running the proverbial Lesia show for decades were at the root of every one of those nagging concerns.

"You're not good enough."

"You're not smart enough."

"You don't have what it takes."

By that time, because I was spending more time writing and speaking, a new belief also vied for my attention: "No one wants to hear what you have to say." And let me tell you, even as I write these words right now, there's a tiny whisper of that belief kickin' around in my mind. However, here I am, writing *anyway*.

A few months into the podcast, I was asked to speak at a Wisdom Women event based out of Los Angeles. Almost immediately, I realized that months of podcasting had provided inspiration for the perfect workshop: "*Who Do You Think You Are?*"—*an engaging, activational opportunity to explore how our thoughts, beliefs, and feelings create our reality, and how ultimately, we are infinitely more powerful, creative, and resilient than anything we could ever think, believe, or feel.*

Much to my delight, the event was a huge success! At the time of writing this book, I've facilitated several more, each time inspiring, engaging, and activating participants to strip away the labels and roles of who they *think* they are and to dig into and explore who and what they *really* are underneath all that. The workshop is also about becoming aware of our *Foundational Life Belief*—the bedrock upon which we've built our life up until now—knowingly or otherwise—and decide whether it's a belief that is helping us to live our most extraordinary life or whether it's keeping us feeling stuck, without knowing how to make a change for the better.

At the beginning of the workshop, I'd share how eagerly Glenn and I anticipated our guests' responses to our question. Because everyone gave the question serious consideration, the answers were as thought-provoking as they were varied. As time went on, one thing became very clear—everyone thought there was something bigger and more profound going on than who they thought themselves to be or what their life experience had been so far. Although each podcast guest responded in their own unique way, at the core, pretty much everyone was saying the same thing. And for me, that was an exciting and fascinating realization.

Now, you can always go and listen to the "Who Do You Think You Are?" podcast episodes for yourself—and I invite you to do so (you can find them on all major podcast platforms and YouTube; just search for Lesia Kohut). However, because I have your undivided attention right now, I'd love to share some of my favourite responses we've gotten to our question so far:

- Craig Lincoln, Olympic bronze medal-winning diver and self-avowed skeptic—"I am a conscious entity. I am a context. I am a con man."
- Archie Tullos, life coach—"I think I knew who I thought I was until you asked me that question … I am more than …"

- Erik Bork, Emmy and Golden Globe Award-winning scriptwriter, author, and spiritual practitioner—"I am not what I appear to be. I am more than I appear. I am not who I think I am."
- Rick Tamlyn, author, activational speaker and coach, co-creator of "The Bigger Game"—"I love your opening…It feels like a game show!"
- Dr. Adrienne McRuvie, chiropractor, doula, yogi, mindfulness teacher—"I am everything, and I am nothing."
- Dr. Ursula Lentine, New Thought minister, pranic healer - "I am a speck of stardust in the infinite reality of the cosmos; I am you; you are me."
- Rev. Patricia Zogar, spiritual leader, Unity Vancouver Island—"I haven't a clue!"

There are so many nuggets of wisdom and insights in every single conversation. As a result, the above responses to that opening question have kept me thinking and wondering as much about who I think myself to be as have my ongoing spiritual/consciousness studies.

How inspiring it has been to hear people from various walks of life, having lived a myriad of life experiences, contributing to the world in their own unique ways, essentially think that who they are is so much more than any label or role we or someone else might ascribe to them. How encouraging it has been to hear guest after guest explain—in their own words—that we are so much bigger than anything we could ever think, believe, or feel. It's no wonder I find myself filled with anticipation and enthusiasm, curious as to how each upcoming guest is going to answer that big, juicy question.

During the editing process of this book, Glenn and I had the opportunity to record a "Who Do You Think You Are?" podcast episode with Dr. Maria Nemeth, personal and financial freedom coach, transformational speaker, and author of *The Energy of Money* and *Mastering Life's Energies*.

I was absolutely thrilled when Maria started off the podcast by saying how much she loved this big question. Why? "Because," she explained, "you can hear it in so many different ways." The first is "just arguing with someone." The second, asking, "Who do you *think* you are—as a *being*?" The third, "Who do you think you *are*?"

Oh my gosh! I was so excited I nearly jumped out of my seat! Here I was, in the middle of editing my book in which I talked about the nuanced meaning of this familiar question depending on which word was emphasized. And here was Maria Nemeth, sharing her interpretations of that question—*based on the same notion.*

One of the things I talk about in the "Who Do You Think You Are?" workshop is the distinction between who we *think* we are vs. who we *truly* are (and sometimes know ourselves to be). This distinction then becomes part of the activational portion of the workshop—where everyone hops into groups of three or four to talk about labels and roles, and look beyond who we think we are. We also end up talking about how our Foundational Life Belief fits in the mix. One of my favourite things to share during the workshop is how I came to discover my Foundational Life Belief.

* * *

One night, early into the year of the inaugural Advanced Consciousness Studies class with Dr. James Mellon and nineteen profoundly brilliant, creative, and engaging minds, he spontaneously asked the class for our Foundational Life Belief. He used his acronym AEP (already established premise). Basically, he wanted to know what the one grounding belief beneath every other belief—the foundation for creating our life experience—was. And he started with me.

Now, even just a few weeks in, I already had serious doubts and reservations about being in this class. From the very first class, I felt like a finger-painting, playing-with-blocks, I-wonder-if-I-can-make-a-record-by-drawing-circles-on-paper-and-putting-it-on-a-record-player-to-play kindergartner in a first-year, university-level class on philosophy and meta- and quantum physics. I felt beyond intimidated and like I really didn't belong there.

To make matters worse, when Dr. James asked me for my AEP, I froze. We're talking deer-in-headlights froze. My eyes were wide open, my mouth agape, and nothing came out. Absolutely *nothing*. It was mortifying.

"Too long. Next!" Within seconds (which felt more like minutes), Dr. James moved on to the next student. As I listened to everyone else in the class share their main belief, what started to bubble up for me came as a big, unwelcome surprise.

"Life is hard."

What? "Life is hard." *That can't be.* "Life is hard." There it was again.

Everyone else in the class was talking about life being an adventure, that it unfolds perfectly, how all their needs are met, to hold things lightly, and more. All I kept hearing in my head was, "Life is hard."

Let me tell you, being in a class filled with practicing New Thought ministers, spiritual practitioners, coaches, and people who'd been immersed in teachings founded in Oneness and the concept of creating our own reality for decades, I already felt uncomfortable. Now that I had four years of intensive spiritual/consciousness studies under my own belt, there was no way I was sharing "Life is hard" with my fellow students.

I knew right away that "Life is hard" was *not* going to be my Foundational Life Belief going forward. Yes, there were many challenges I'd overcome in my life, but just because things had been tough before, didn't necessarily mean they had to be tough going forward. "Life is hard" just wasn't going to work, and I knew I'd have to allow for something different to take its place.

For the next few weeks, I thought about what my Foundational Life Belief could be. There were plenty of beliefs that would come up, but none of them felt infinitely life-affirming and expansive. None of them felt like they were that one "desert island" belief that could be the activational taproot of my entire life experience going forward. One day, while writing a thought paper for that same class, I found myself writing about something new.

"There is always more…" *Hmmm, interesting.* "There is always more…" *That feels good.* "There is always more…" *I think this is the one!*

There is always more to learn. There is always more to discover. There is always more to lean into, to be expanded by. There is always more to embrace and embody. There is always more money, time, and energy. There is always more love, laughter, and joy.

There is always more…

The list went on and on, and I felt like my heart was going to explode with joy! "There is always more…" had cemented itself as my Foundational Life Belief. This was the one belief that was underneath and behind every other belief. So no matter how icky and yucky some of those other beliefs could sometimes feel (hello, "You're not good enough," "You're not smart enough," "You don't have what it takes," and "No one wants to hear what you have to say"), now that I was firmly founded and grounded in "There is always more…" I felt empowered. I felt enlivened. I felt emboldened, and ready to say, "F*&% you!" to any other limiting belief that might want my attention because I knew, at the very core of my soul, *"There is always more… "*

A few weeks later, during a teacher training with Dr. James, I had another opportunity to share my Foundational Life Belief. This time, I was ready. What was even more amazing was that as I was listening to others share their AEP's, another voice started up in my head. This time, it wasn't one of my usual (suspect) beliefs; it was the voice of my friend Archie ("Who do you Think you Are?" podcast guest #6) and his response to our podcast question.

In that moment, my Foundational Life Belief—which already felt rock-solid—expanded into, "There is always more, *and I am always more than…*" I didn't even hear what most of the other participants offered up, I was so excited to share my newly revised

AEP. Not only is there always more to life than who I think myself to be or what I may be experiencing, but regardless of who I think myself to be, or what I may be experiencing, I am *always* more than that. I am more than my thoughts, my beliefs, feelings, and my experiences. I am more than anything I could ever think, believe, or feel—more than *anything* I could ever experience!

As I began to realize these things for myself, I also began to realize that my relationship with my dad had been so much more than what it had appeared to be. I came to realize that my bakery experience had been so much more meaningful than the epic financial failure and emotional roller coaster it had felt like for so long. I also came to realize that the intoxicating siren call of moving across country was about so much more than a calmer, cleaner, healthier way of living or of being surrounded by nature.

I began to realize that each of these experiences was part of the deepening transition from awareness to understanding and now realization. This deepening transition opened and continues to open my eyes, mind, and heart to me seeing myself for who I truly am, and not who I previously thought or even believed myself to be.

The more consciously I embrace this true identity, the more I am able to move forward in life embodying who I know myself to be, rather than who I may have thought myself to be until now.

Chapter 7

A Shift in Perspective, A Shift in Power

"The boy reached through to the Soul of the World and saw that it was a part of the Soul of God. And he saw that the Soul of God was his own soul. And that he, a boy, could perform miracles."

– Paul Coelho, *The Alchemist*

In her best-selling book *Big Magic*, Elizabeth Gilbert devotes a portion of the chapter "Courage" to a list of potential fears. She writes about being afraid of not having any talent, of being rejected or ignored. She writes about being afraid that somebody else may be doing something better or more quickly than you, or that if you unleash your talent and wisdom into the world, someone might come along and steal it.

When I look at the pages-long list of fears in her book—seeing several I can relate to all too well—what I see is a list of beliefs founded in fear. Underneath every one of these beliefs, however, is another deeply rooted belief: "I'm not good enough" or "I don't matter." And, when "I'm not good enough" or "I don't matter" are running the show, it doesn't matter how many affirmations you repeat or self-help books you read or "Embrace Your Power" webinars you attend. Until you let go of those beliefs you've been holding onto so dearly for so long, life won't change very much. Or if it does, the change won't last.

Why? Because even though on the surface you've set some goals, made some lifestyle changes, and have taken some action, you're still rooted—even *entangled*— in the same beliefs that have kept you feeling stuck for most of your life. So, no matter how many times you suck it up and put on a positive face, you're basically doomed to repeat the life you've been living—perhaps with some different clothes, a different partner, a different home, even a different career—but still with those same nagging, anxiety-inducing thoughts and limitations you've been living with up until now. And hear me when I say, these beliefs will continue to be the boss of you, until you begin to live life from a new set of beliefs.

One of the biggest shifts in perception for me was during my first year of Spiritual Practitioner Studies as we were reading Thomas Moore's *Care of the Soul*. That book remains my favourite of that first year, and at the time, was so impactful that our weekly Sunday study group became affectionately known as "Care of the Soil." The "soil" part came from a commonly used gardening metaphor that is used in the Science of Mind teachings to describe the creative process—how we create our life experience. One of the biggest "aha" moments I've had to this day came as I was reading the section on failure.

Every week, in addition to the assigned readings and other homework, Dr. James would also ask us to bring to class at least one salient point from each chapter/source we'd read that week to discuss. With *Care of the Soul* it seemed there were always several to choose from. When it came to the section on failure, however, there was a portion of a paragraph that leapt out at me:

> *"By appreciating failure with imagination, we reconnect it to success. Without the connection, work falls into grand narcissistic fantasies of success and dismal feelings of failure. But as a mystery, failure is not mine, it is an element in the work I am doing."*

"(F)ailure is not mine, it is an element in the work I am doing." I have since come to paraphrase this statement as "Failure is not who or what I am, it is an element of the work I do."

As soon as I saw failure in this new light, my entire relationship with it—my perspective—shifted. And not just in my current relationship, but how I viewed failures in the past and what failure might mean in the future. As my relationship with failure itself shifted, so did my perception of my relationship with my dad and with the unfolding of circumstances around my bakery. This was an actual revelation to me—one that has and continues to have an enormous impact on how I show up in the world and how I approach the work I now do. Thanks to that one incredible insight, my perspective on failure completely changed.

Did that mean that the pain, anger, and fear I'd felt for so many years because of the tenuous relationship with my dad instantly went away? No. Did it mean the heart-wrenching, exhausting, and monumentally challenging times during the opening and closing of my bakery didn't actually happen? Not at all.

It was more like when we moved to Victoria to start a new life. Even though we felt pain, anger, and fear; even though we felt immersed in shame, embarrassment, and humiliation in asking our friends for money only two months after our move; even though there were days when we felt like we'd made a huge mistake, by that time we *knew* that it was all part of the work we were doing.

That shift in perception of failure grounded us in the knowing that—no matter how much life seemed to suck at the moment— we were exactly where we were meant to be. Regardless of what was going on and what we were feeling, we were moving our feet, taking tiny baby step after tiny baby step while moving forward in the direction of our dreams.

Another significant shift in perception that has really helped me in recent years is also courtesy of Thomas Moore: "finding the sacred in everything we do." Moore says that by beginning to view life differently—by shifting our perception, which then allows us to see life from a new perspective—we open ourselves up to the beauty, wonder, and exhilaration of life in everyone and everything, including in the most mundane of tasks.

This reminds me of a Sunday talk at the Centre for Spiritual Living Toronto during which Rev. Jonathan talked about his distaste for bookkeeping, but that it was something that had to be done, nonetheless. One day, instead of grumbling about having to do the work, he decided to find the joy and value in the task instead, ultimately making it more enjoyable and getting the work done more quickly.

The idea of mindfully revering even the most tedious of tasks was also what inspired me to shift my perception of my work as a grocery store associate shortly after moving to Victoria. In purposefully finding the joy and value in what I was doing, I discovered how meditative and calming it could be. I realized what a relief it was to actually be in an environment where there was so much order, while my home was still filled with moving boxes and in a state of chaos.

Today, one of my favourite things to do is hang laundry in my backyard. Taking the damp, crumpled balls of fabric, mindfully untangling them into their proper forms, hanging them on the drying rack or laundry line, choosing very purposefully where to pin the clothes pegs so they don't leave a noticeable dent in the clothing once dried while breathing in the warm summer air, revelling in the farmland, ocean, and mountains around me, is embracing the sacred in the mundane. It's finding the joy and value in an otherwise not-so-inspiring chore.

It wasn't always this way. It took energy, attention, and focus along with being willing to look at an obligatory task in a new and different way. It took practice. And when I say "practice," I'm using it as a noun *and* a verb. Practice is an activity. Practice is ongoing. Now, hanging laundry continues to be one of my favourite spiritual or mindfulness practices.

Finding the sacred in the mundane is very personal and can look completely different for you than it does for me. It can also look different tomorrow than it does today. Regardless, engaging in some form of mindful or spiritual practice—finding the joy and value in everything we do—allows us to open ourselves up to seeing ourselves and the world in new ways. It allows us to shift our perception so we can view life from a different and new perspective.

We are not our thoughts. We are not our beliefs. We are not our feelings. We are God/Energy/Love—whatever is meaningful for you—*in action.* Who and What we are is what inspires all thoughts, beliefs, and feelings—of all time. We are infinite possibilities in action. When we view the world from this perspective, we can finally see ourselves as the Infinite Creative Energy we are, and that we are unstoppable!

We create our life experience based on the thoughts, beliefs, and feelings we identify with the most. If those thoughts, beliefs, and feelings have you living the life of your dreams—awesome! If not, perhaps now's the time to become aware of what thoughts, beliefs, and feelings are keeping you living a life that's less than awesome. Remember, you are always choosing from that never-ending buffet of infinite possibilities. So why not choose something different and new?

As you begin to take a more active role in choosing what to think, what to believe, and how to feel, you'll come to understand that not only do you have a hand in creating your life experience, *you are the hand.*

So I say, wade into the muck and dig in!

Start unearthing those limiting beliefs that have kept you feeling overwhelmed and stuck in pain, anger, fear, anxiety, confusion, and low self-esteem—even mediocrity or apathy. Open up your mind, heart, and soul to seeing the world in a new and different light—from a new, more empowering set of beliefs.

The more you stop identifying with the limiting beliefs you've been holding onto for so long, the more you'll begin to realize how infinitely powerful, creative, and resilient you are. Once you begin to see life from this new empowered perspective, the more you'll be able to embody—to live from and as—the Infinite Power, Creativity, and Resilience you are. The more you'll be able to live from and as the Infinite Power, Creativity, and Resilience *you've been all along.*

Section 3

Discovery
(Treasure)

Chapter 8

Spiritual Principles and Quantum Realizations

"(W)e ourselves are not a discrete reference point or an "I" separate from the process of the endless becoming of the universe. The universe, like a never-ending work of art, is a work-in-progress in which we ourselves are participating every moment, dreaming it up while simultaneously being dreamed up by it."

– Paul Levy, *The Quantum Revelation*

In late April 2020, we wrote our final exam for Spiritual Practitioner Studies. Even though I had studied and felt totally confident going into the exam, the exam experience itself left me feeling anything but. It had been a gruelling three-hour ordeal that had tested us on pretty much everything we'd learned, not only during our most recent two years in Spiritual Practitioner Studies, but also what we *might have* learned in the two years of prerequisite study leading up to the practitioner program. I was amazed that some of my fellow classmates managed to finish in just over an hour, while I ended up using every second of that exam time to first answer what came easily and then to read and reread the remaining questions. Eventually, I ended up sitting quietly. Determined to not leave any question unanswered, I endeavoured to tap into the intuitive knowing that all the answers I required were within me. As we'd been taught more than a few times during our years of study: *The same mind taking the exam, is the same mind that wrote the exam.*

After class that night, I felt relieved. The hard part was over. Now, there were just the oral panels. And, for me, they were going to be a piece of cake!

Later that night, however, I dreamt about the exam. The next morning—after having dreamt about the exam throughout the night—I found myself questioning several of my answers. The more I second-guessed myself, the more convinced I became that I may have actually failed the exam. And the more I felt I may have failed it, the more unravelled I became.

If I had failed my written exam, I wouldn't be allowed to take my oral panels. If I couldn't take my orals, it would mean I wouldn't pass. If I didn't pass, I wouldn't be able to officially do the work I'd come to love and had been training for these last four years. And more importantly, it would mean I wouldn't be going into ministerial studies the following year, which had been my goal and the trajectory I'd been on for nearly half a decade.

Although I tried so hard not to get caught up in "maybes" and "what ifs," there were several times throughout the day during which I'd have to excuse myself from work and go cry outside or in the washroom because of the overwhelming sense of failure

I felt. Even though I had come to understand that "failure" was not Who and What I am, but an element of the work I do, it still felt like my world was falling apart. By the time I got home that evening, all I could do was walk up our front stairs, through the living room and kitchen, out onto the deck, collapse into a chair, and just sob.

It was as if I'd stepped into a parallel universe or alternate reality. It felt as if the most agonizing pain body—the excruciating anguish and torment of a lifetime of trapped pain and trauma (mine *and* the world's)—was erupting to the surface all at once. The surge was so overwhelming and so overpowering, the only thing I could do was go along for the ride. And smack dab in the middle of that emotional onslaught were—with a renewed sense of vim and vigor—the three main beliefs that I had worked so hard to let go of during my Soul Excavation of the past four years.

"You're not good enough."

"You're not smart enough."

"You don't have what it takes."

The gamut of feelings I experienced transcended mere pain. This was anguish, torment, and despair. This was a complete tearing apart, breaking down, and full-on annihilation of whatever confidence I may have felt just the day before or who I had thought myself to be until that moment. It was Humpty Dumpty's final fall off the proverbial wall, with me smashing to smithereens on the ground below.

As the waves of agony and seeming defeat grew in intensity, I felt *everything* in every part of my body. Even though there was a part of me that could see I was spiralling into a destructive, self-fulfilling prophecy, there was another part of me that also knew I had to live through whatever was happening. In that excruciating whirlwind of failure, I could feel myself bereft over not having what it would take to be a spiritual practitioner. In that grief, lay the proof that I wasn't good enough or smart enough, period.

As intense as this experience was, however, I knew this was growth and (r)evolution happening hard and fast. I knew I had to face those beliefs head-on, right there and then. By the end of that evening, I felt completely wrung out and exhausted.

A few days later, we received our marks from Dr. James, and admittedly, I was completely shocked when I saw my mark: I'd scored in the high 90s. I found myself wondering, *Is this a mistake?* It was as if I'd written a completely different exam from the one Dr. James had graded. However, with that shock also came relief. And even though it took a few days to bounce back from the emotional roller coaster and alternate reality of a few nights before, the excitement and enthusiasm for our upcoming oral panels began to bubble up.

The day of my oral panels for Spiritual Practitioner Studies was one of the most memorable, joy-filled days of my life so far. The eight remaining members of our tightly knit, profoundly interconnected collective had each been assigned a specific time when were supposed to sign on to the Zoom call. Once we were in the room, Dr. James would observe off-screen as the panel of two ordained New Thought ministers and one licensed spiritual practitioner (who was just weeks away from becoming a New Thought minister herself) asked their questions and posed their challenges to confirm whether or not we were ready to become licensed as religious science practitioners.

I was the second in our class to go, and after just over thirty minutes of engaging, joyful, fun, and easy breezy conversation along with a couple of super activational Spiritual Mind Treatments, I was given a resounding, unanimous, "Yes, yes, yes!" After getting off the call, I literally jumped for joy!

Here's the thing, though. It hadn't come as a surprise at all because earlier that day, during the series of morning meditations I'd engaged in, I had actually *experienced* passing my orals—mentally, emotionally, spiritually, and physically. I felt completely elevated and expanded and floated out of that morning meditation with a massive perma-grin on my face and celebration in my soul! I had already experienced the successful outcome, so going through the oral panels experience was a mere formality.

I immediately sent an en masse email to everyone in the class to let them know I'd passed. Within minutes, the classmate who'd gone before me wrote that she too had passed. As the day continued, almost everyone in the class chimed in numerous times to congratulate and cheer one another on. Over the course of the day and into the evening, I felt so incredibly in love with and interconnected to these beautiful, brilliant beings. I felt so fully immersed in this expansive experience and so in tune with the joyful, creative, magnificent unfoldment of life itself. I was also ready to burst because I was just a couple of months away from beginning ministerial studies in the fall.

A few weeks later, along with many from the Global Truth Center Los Angeles community, I cheered online as I watched Dr. James's ministerial class give their "Ten Talks." They were just days away from their oral panels, and their TEDx-like talks were one of the final requirements before their panels.

With each successive speaker, the joy, wisdom, inspiration, and love from the event emanated through my screen. With each successive introduction, Dr. James would share how much he loved and was inspired by each of these brilliant, expansive minds as they brought their unique ministries into the world.

In the middle of one of his introductions, immersed in that palpable joy, wisdom, inspiration, and love, Dr. James paused. And in less than a split second, I knew what he was about to say.

With great reverence, gratitude, and love he commented on what an extraordinary class this had been and how journeying with this particular collective had so incredibly surpassed his expectations. And because this experience was ending on such a high note, he didn't think he could ever teach a better ministerial class. He announced right there and then that he was done. He wouldn't be teaching ministerial studies again. In the midst of all that joy, wisdom, inspiration, and love, my heart sank.

* * *

"(I)nstead of unthinkingly taking on others' ideas about who we are, we should, based on our own experience, find out for ourselves."
    – Paul Levy, *The Quantum Revelation*

In September of 2020, after much deliberation and with no small amount of trepidation, I attended Dr. James Mellon's very first Advanced Consciousness Studies class, accredited by the

Emerson Theological Institute. Although it had been decided by Dr. James and Dr. Angelo Pizelo, the dean of the Emerson Institute, that this class would count as first-year ministerial studies for me, I still felt disappointed that I wasn't in for the experience I'd been expecting and looking forward to for the past four years. Equally discombobulating was feeling that everyone else in the class was so much further ahead on their spiritual journeys than I, and that I really didn't even belong there.

From the very beginning, Dr. James shared how this class was not a class, that he wasn't our teacher, and that he was along for the meta and quantum physical ride of exploring "What is Consciousness?" right along with us. Even though it took me nearly three-quarters of the year—kicking and screaming most of the time—I eventually reached the point where not only did I feel like I belonged, but that this immersive experience had so incredibly surpassed my expectations of what year one of ministerial studies was supposed to look like that I was actually more prepared for my evolving ministry than I would've been had I ventured down the more recognized ministerial path.

I came into the Advanced Consciousness Studies class thinking I had a firm grasp on the Science of Mind teachings and the meaning of concepts like truth, love, spirituality, consciousness, and even reality. I came in thinking I understood what the creative process was all about, and that because I'd been immersed in four intensive years of spiritual/consciousness studies that this year's class would simply be an extension of what I already knew.

We began with Plato's allegory *The Cave*—a story of perception, ignorance, belief, and truth, which also deals with the notion that the curious and enlightened are often ridiculed or dismissed when trying to share their newfound wisdom. We then moved on to learning about the distinction between brain and mind, including the physical and chemical effects of mindfulness in *Buddha's Brain* by Dr. Rick Hansen.

When I saw *Buddha's Brain* on our reading list, I had a feeling it was already in our book collection. I searched for it for weeks without any luck. When Dr. James finally announced—during our first class—that we'd begin discussing it the following week, I asked Glenn if he'd seen it anywhere. He said, "No."

Still convinced we had it, I kept looking. Eventually, I found it, sitting behind some other books. It was brand-spankin'-new and hadn't been read yet. When I looked inside, I beamed. I found a bookmark from a bookstore *in Victoria* from the first summer we visited and felt called to move. I'd bought the book in Victoria, it had come back to Toronto with us, and then made the move across country two years later to end up being part of a class I was in *five years later.*

After *Buddha's Brain,* we dipped our proverbial toes into the infinite sea of quantum physics, quantum activism, and the various aspects of consciousness with Amit Goswami's *The Everything Answer Book.* We then explored Sasha Sagan's *For Small Creatures Such as We* on ritual and meaning—a light, refreshing palate cleanser of sorts—before heading full tilt into the quantum realm, having our individual and collective minds blown wide open with Paul Levy's *The Quantum Revelation.* Where Amit Goswami endeavoured to provide answers to some of life's biggest questions like "Who are we?" "What is consciousness?" "What happens when we die?" Paul Levy opened the floodgate of never-ending questions as he offered his interpretation of quantum theory as it relates to reality, time, oneness, and yes...consciousness.

By the time we finished with *What Is Consciousness?* by Jean Houston, Larry Dossey, and Ervin Laszlo—a collection of essays sharing the authors' views on this heady topic—not only had my first-year ministerial studies not looked like what I had it expected to, but this Advanced Consciousness Studies class had just blown to smithereens the very foundation that had been cemented with Spiritual Practitioner Studies less than a year earlier.

I had gone from being moored in absolute certainty to feeling completely untethered, in a constant state of curiosity, confusion, and questioning—all at once. I didn't know what I believed anymore and ended up feeling uneasy to the point of nausea and anxiety for most of the year. Eventually, however, I discovered that living in the fluidity and wonder of ever-evolving mystery was actually a pretty amazing place to be.

The unofficial motto of our class was: "Question everything!" And question everything we did. The other unofficial motto was something akin to: "There are no words." The more we tried to explain or describe what we were learning about and experiencing, the more it became consensus that words or language ended up limiting the limitless.

I think that on some level, the latter is true. However, I also think that in endeavouring to describe something as heady as consciousness, God, Spirit, or even Love (note the capital "L"), trying to do so with words invites us to push ourselves out of our comfort zones, away from the familiar and into the unknown.

It's an opportunity to move beyond what we have already experienced, to reach beyond our immediate grasp, to stretch beyond what we already know and to consciously, intentionally, and purposefully open ourselves up to that infinite potentiality of the quantum field. It's a way to try to express the ineffable. Isn't this what poets, bards, musicians, and authors have been doing since time immemorial...?

* * *

"When we are face to face with truth, the point of view of Krishna, Buddha, Christ, or any other prophet is the same. When we look at life from the top of the mountain, there is no limitation; there is the same immensity."

– Hazrat Inayat Khan

When I officially began my spiritual journey, I was taught that there are universal principles or truths—steadfast, concrete, and inarguable—that are the same for everyone. I was taught that these truths are what we find in the words, poems, and teachings of the great mystics and that they transcend time and space. After Advanced Consciousness Studies, however, my understanding of truth has evolved.

If the Universe is constantly recreating and rebooting itself every moment of every day, if the quantum field is infinite potentiality, then the only thing that is constant is *change*. Even that observation is based on what is known, understood, and in how we observe, measure, express, and quantify things—as of this moment.

Quantum physics also tells us that there is no self-existing, generating reality outside of our own experience. I suppose this could be considered a truth—for now. If we're all indeed creating our own realities, would it not stand to reason that there could be my truth, your truth, or even various collective agreed-upon truths? And are they indeed unwavering and steadfast or are they changeable and ever-evolving, just like we are?

I believe there are spiritual principles that stand up to the variability and infinite potentiality of quantum physics, remaining steadfast, concrete, and inarguable—for now. I also believe that when they're really felt and embodied at one's very core, these principles become a *spiritual realization*. The thing is—perhaps because the Universe is always changing and we as expressions of the Universe are at different levels of awareness at any given moment—not all principles resonate with everyone all the time. They can sound good, even make sense. But if a principle falls flat, if you can't *feel* it in every fibre of your being, it'll be impossible to anchor yourself in it.

One common principle in the Science of Mind teachings is: "Life is always unfolding perfectly." It speaks to the mathematical certainty and order of life. For a lot of people, it works. For me, not so much.

The reason I'm not super hyped about "Life is always unfolding perfectly" is because life doesn't always feel peachy keen. For some, the word "perfect" is just too charged, and as such, can backfire, seemingly resulting in the opposite of the intended effect. The irony is that even when life feels like a bitch, it's still unfolding perfectly—exactly according to our "Life's a bitch" beliefs.

For me, although I get it, I don't *feel* it. While it may be a spiritual principle that is always in play, because it doesn't resonate, it doesn't work as a spiritual realization I can anchor myself in.

When comparing what quantum physics reveals with what poets, artists, and mystics have experienced through the ages, there seems to be a truth that is fundamental to and for all. This is what Hazrat Inayat Khan's simple, yet profound quote at the beginning of this section speaks to with such poignancy. That no matter where we come from or how we perceive the world, beneath those perceptions, there is only one foundational truth that interconnects and is the inception of us all.

In viewing the world through this expanded quantum lens, I still find myself turning to certain spiritual principles. They help me make sense out of life, they inspire, and they further ground me in a truth that feels rock-solid for me—that there is one Universal Energetic Flow that is the essence of all being, of all time, and that everyone and everything is a unique, original expression of that Flow. Anchoring myself in spiritual realization opens me up to what's possible rather than what's probable.

One such principle—my absolute fave and one that resonates more than any other when I'm working with clients—is: "Principle is not bound by precedent," coined by Thomas Troward.

It means that there is absolutely nothing that has ever happened (precedent) that could ever have any bearing on Who and What you truly are (principle). If you (principle) drag something from the past (precedent) into the present moment with you, you may *feel* affected by the past. However, as an expression of the Infinite Energetic Flow that is the essence of everyone and everything, you remain as powerful and resilient as ever—*no matter what.*

When looking at this principle from a quantum perspective, the meaning of it expands even further because in the quantum realm, there is no time or space. So, the value in this principle extends not only to the past, but to the future as well. Nothing that has ever happened or could happen has any bearing on Who and What you are. *No one. No thing. No thought, belief, or feeling. No expectation. No circumstance. No diagnosis. No experience ever* can or *will* diminish the Infinite Creativity, Resilience, and Love that each and every one of us is at our core.

Yet another is: "Our outer world reflects our inner world." Which, ironically, says the same thing as "Life is always unfolding perfectly." When worded this way, however, this principal *does* land for me. I *feel* it in my body. I *see* it in my relationships. I *experience* it in life all around me. It's a spiritual realization I can fully anchor myself in. And I do.

This realization causes me to question and re-evaluate my thoughts about, resulting behaviour, and contribution to relationships and events going on around me. It reminds me that even if I didn't necessarily cause something to happen, I was, at the very least, at the level of awareness of attracting it into my orb. I'm reminded that I create my reality according to what I choose to think, believe, and feel. If I don't like what's happening or how I'm behaving, I get to think, believe, and/or feel something different, thereby changing my experience. This realization also reminds me to be patient and compassionate with others because we're all vibrating at a certain level of awareness at any given time and we're not always resonating at the same frequency.

Another common spiritual principle—one that I also find incredibly empowering—is: "We are always at choice." Learning that I—not some external force or entity—am mistress of my destiny and that nothing is written in stone was as liberating as it was enlightening. I have come to know that not only are we always at choice, but we are also always *choosing*. Sometimes we choose by design (knowingly), sometimes by default (unknowingly).

In *The Quantum Revelation*, Paul Levy writes, "The more often a particular perception takes place, the more deeply it is imprinted into our unconscious, and hence, the more likely it is to reoccur in the future." This can be taken as a blessing or a curse. We can choose to stick with those perceptions or the tendencies of thought that can keep us feeling stuck in a repetitive loop of more of what we've experienced so far. Or we can change our tendency of thought by *consciously* choosing to focus on thoughts, beliefs, and feelings that are more life-affirming, expansive, and free us up to live the life we want. We can either live by design or by default. The choice is ours.

As someone who felt like I'd lived according to other people's rules and expectations for most of my life, this principle felt incredibly empowering and activational when I first heard it.

To realize that even if circumstances around me didn't change, that I could change my perception of or relationship to those circumstances—just by changing how I think about those circumstances—meant I was in control of my life, not someone else. Even if those grooves of perception were so deeply ingrained it felt like there was no way to skip out of them or create a new groove, I was still the one who was choosing to stay stuck, not someone else. I am always able to choose something different, and in choosing, I am always creating a new life experience for myself— every single moment, of every single day. It's what's happening.

We can also delve even further into this principle, taking into consideration the infinite nature of the quantum field. Not only can I pivot in another direction by choosing to think something different, but I can also feel or experience something different. How? By leaping into or drawing from another reality. Yes, you heard me. Just like in the German Netflix mini-series, *Dark*, or the movie *Sliding Doors* or an episode of *Star Trek: The Next Generation*, we can actually do the seemingly impossible—even illogical—just by using our minds. Why? Because of three very important quantum realizations:

- **Everyone creates their reality.** There is no separate reality occurring outside of what we experience as our reality, even though the things and circumstances of life make a very convincing argument otherwise. This means that even if we appear to have a collective experience with others, every individual experience is different because everyone is creating their own version of the agreed-upon collective reality.

- **There are infinite realities that can be potentially experienced at any given time.** The quantum field is filled with infinite possibilities, and because it is not bound by time or space, all possible realities—past, present, and future—occur simultaneously, which means, any of them can be experienced *in the present moment.*

Is it magic? Not really, even though it might feel like it. Is it easy? Not necessarily, but it can be. Can anyone do it? Totally!

The more we consciously practice focusing our attention on what's possible, rather than what's probable, the more we

create new grooves or new trajectories for us to experience—
as we're creating them. This is how the probable becomes
the inevitable. It's the alchemical magic of mysticism and
the wonder of science coming together as the exciting,
exhilarating practice of living from the unknown of Infinite
Possibilities.

- **Even though it may appear to be, reality is not constant.**
The Universe is refreshing and rebooting itself anew—as
are we ourselves—every moment of every day. Every single
now moment is a brand-spankin'-new opportunity of life
and living.

Why is this important? Because again, it shows how each and every
one of us is in charge of our life experience—we and no one else.
For me, when those usual (suspect) beliefs of "You're not good
enough," "You're not smart enough," and "You don't have what it
takes" pop up, every single moment is a brand new opportunity
to remember that what I focus on expands (another great spiritual
principle, by the way), and where I put my attention, I put my
energy. I get to consider whether I want to focus on beliefs that
make me feel "less than" or whether I want to shift my gaze to
more life-affirming and expansive beliefs like, "You are infinitely
more powerful, creative, and resilient than anything that you
could ever think, believe, or feel—*than anything you could ever
experience.*"

A quantum perspective, like spiritual principle, opens us up to
realizing that we aren't relegated to some predetermined or fated
trajectory. Rather, we can consciously choose to draw from
another trajectory (a desire, vision, or sleeping dream) to make

the one we're currently on more desirable. Or we can become so in tune with the infinite creativity we are at our core that we can actually *leap* from our current reality to a different reality just by changing our thoughts, or even our perceptions of the reality we are seemingly experiencing in a certain moment. *Nothing is set in stone, even if it appears otherwise.* Just because something happened a certain way before, doesn't mean it has to happen like that again.

* * *

"It is traumatic to realize that the world that we thought we lived in doesn't exist in the way we thought it did...When we discover something that so completely changes and rocks our world, we can easily find ourselves disoriented, experiencing a shock that needs time to be metabolized, digested, and integrated."
– Paul Levy, *The Quantum Revelation*

Even with spiritual realizations and their newly revised quantum interpretations, life can still feel like a tangled, confusing mess— especially as we endeavour to embody a quantum worldview while still seemingly embracing a classical life experience. I think that discombobulating, disconcerting, and sometimes painful expansion is illustrated so perfectly in the above quote by Paul Levy.

So how do we live from the infinite potentiality of the quantum field where there is no time and space while seemingly navigating a more classical world where we feel continually bound by time and space? How do we move away from creating our life from the known and allow ourselves to venture into the unknown? How do we move beyond our comfort zones into the infinite, untapped possibilities of the new? This is where one of my favourite new phrases, "Trouble at the border," comes into play.

A variation on what Paul Levy refers to as "border trouble"—the border between the classical and quantum worlds—"Trouble at the border" is a phrase used by *The Energy of Money* author Dr. Maria Nemeth.

In her book and trainings on financial and personal freedom, she uses this phrase to indicate the point we reach as we get ready to step out of our comfort zones or where we are (what she calls "physical reality") to who we truly are and what we are capable of and meant to be ("visionary reality"). As we reach the border, we are met with what Nemeth and Buddhists refer to as "Monkey Mind"—those limiting thoughts, beliefs, feelings, and excuses that will continually, incessantly vie for our attention by trying to convince us that it makes more sense to stay right where we are rather than to venture over the border into unknown territory.

Another term for this? Ego. If it were up to ego—whose job it is to keep us safe—we might never actually experience anything new. In her book *The Energy Codes*, Dr. Sue Morter writes that when it comes to living a life based exclusively from ego, "(T)his protective approach to life tends to limit what we are willing to try, because 'safety' is its first priority. This makes our relationships with others very conditional, keeps us off-balance, and creates continual stress that eventually take a major toll, mentally, emotionally, and physically."

When it comes to "Trouble at the border," the idea is to acknowledge our ego or "Monkey Mind," tap into our innate authenticity, and move across the border *anyway* so that we can begin creating our life from and as that Universal Energetic Flow that is infinite in scope and creative by nature. Life beyond our comfort zone—the new and unknown—is where the excitement lies. Navigating "Trouble at the Border" despite the incessant chatter of "Monkey Mind" or the instinctive, protective impulse of ego is how we shift from living as who we've understood ourselves to be so far to living as Who and What we are meant to be.

Just as Nemeth talks about how important it is to acknowledge "Monkey Mind" and keep moving over the border anyway, what I have found regarding the quantum/classical conundrum is that it is imperative to consciously live from a quantum perspective, while and in spite of navigating the classical realm. It's not a "this or that" kind of situation, it's "both and." These are two different ways of looking at the world that don't have to be mutually exclusive. The more we acknowledge, cultivate, and nurture them both, the more interesting and engaging life can become—at least that's how I see it.

Spiritual principles lay the groundwork for realizing that we aren't relegated to some predetermined or fated trajectory. They are the invitation, inspiration, and affirmation that we are each in charge of creating our own reality and that we are so much more infinitely powerful, creative, and resilient than anything we could ever think, feel, believe, or experience. They are also a reminder that beneath every personal view, there is an underlying current of truth that unites and interconnects us all.

When spiritual principles land and we begin to embody them with every fibre of our being, they become a spiritual realization—an impulse that activates and elevates our creativity from and as the Infinite Creativity, Resilience, and Love we are rather than circumstances in our life. Quantum realizations (for me) are the brilliant aha's and nuggets of wisdom that come from the conscious immersion in and cultivation and embodiment of spiritual realizations. They are the constant invitation to move beyond what we have known and experienced so far—an opportunity to open up to what's possible instead of what's probable. They are the portal to plunging into the untapped creativity and activity of living the most engaging, fulfilling, vibrant life that is ours to live.

As we continue through our individual Soul Excavation, the Soul Excavation of the world occurs as well. As we dig, unearth, and explore, we are always at opportunity to discover that we are not separate from the rest of the universe. In doing so, we become more imbued with *Divine Intertwinglement* that keeps us all interconnected, inspired, and activated as the Infinite Creativity, Resilience, and Love we truly are.

Chapter 9

Divine Intertwinglement

"(A)s each of us expands our conscious light of self-reflective awareness, the whole universe shines that much brighter."
– Paul Levy, *The Quantum Revelation*

One of the challenges that kept coming up during my year in the Advanced Consciousness Studies class was language. More specifically, the challenge was in how to describe or talk about big, ineffable concepts like truth, oneness, God, and consciousness. The bigger the concept, the more words it took to come to the conclusion that there are no words accurate enough to explain the unexplainable. Why? Because words and language are human constructs that limit concepts and ideas to mere descriptions of what they are, rather than what they truly are. As such, by using words to try and explain the meaning of truth, oneness, God, and consciousness, all we were doing was limiting the limitless. Or were we?

I believe words can be limiting. I also believe words can be liberating. I believe endeavouring to explain something as mind-bending and seemingly ineffable as oneness using only words can feel daunting. However, I also believe we should still try. Why? Because when we realize we can't rely on what we have in front of us, we are pushed, inspired, even activated to move *beyond* the limitations of our current understanding and capability. That inspiration opens us up to stepping out of our comfort zones, which in turn allows us to gain new insights and perspectives on what it is we're trying to understand. These new insights and perspectives are what ignites our imagination and allows us to more fully experience the Infinite Creativity, Resilience, and Love we innately are and what we can become. Words may be limiting by nature, but language is continually expanding and evolving out of necessity, *as are we.*

* * *

My first encounter with Dr. James Mellon was through the Centre for Spiritual Living Toronto, just a few months before we moved to Victoria. The community was all abuzz because he was coming up for Rev. Jonathan's ordination in a few weeks.

Dr. James had been Rev. Jonathan's teacher and mentor for many years. While in Toronto, he would also be performing a one-man show, *Sissy Boy*. The promo image in the Centre flyer looked bizarre, even slightly disturbing, and I—being new to the community—wasn't sure what to make of him or his play.

In our brief time at CSL Toronto, Dr. James had been quoted numerous times during Sunday Celebration with his book and 16-week mindset-shifting bootcamp *Mental Muscle*, being an abundance of inspiration. When people talked about him, it was with extreme reverence and enthusiasm. Other than that, I had no idea who he was.

When I finally heard him speak at Rev. Jonathan's ordination a few weeks later, I was amazed. He was articulate, smart, witty, and extremely entertaining. During the potluck celebration afterward, however, the extent of my interaction with Dr. James was him asking me about a couple of dishes in the buffet and whether or not they were vegetarian. At the time, I had no idea that his presence in my life would play such an integral role in my understanding and embodiment of mind-boggling concepts like truth, oneness, God, and consciousness—and Love.

* * *

When I first started tuning in to the Global Truth Center Los Angeles (GTC for short) Sunday celebrations online, I was delighted to find them more akin to a concert or television production with live music, guest speakers, and an extremely engaging, charismatic, entertaining, sometimes self-indulgent, captivating leading man. It was clear that Dr. James's background had been in musical theatre and the performing arts, and it didn't take long before a Broadway reference—or two or three or four—made it into the celebration. When it came to "Enlightenment Through Entertainment"—Dr. James's motto—he and the GTC Sunday Celebrations totally, 100 percent delivered.

One Sunday during my second year of Spiritual Practitioner Studies, I was tuned in to the online GTC Celebration. During that talk, Dr. James tripped over a word, and out came "Intertwingle." In true Dr. James fashion, he made a joke of it, laughed it off, and kept on going. For me, though, the word stuck.

Intertwingle. I loved it.

I loved the way it sounded. I loved the way it rolled off the tongue. I loved how it made me *feel*. I loved that it conjured up so many images and feelings all at once, and it had just spontaneously been blurted out in error. Or had it?

For me, there was no error. That word stuck like glue and kept popping into my mind, into my purview for days, even weeks after that talk. Lingering, expanding, inspiring. After a while, I couldn't remember the talk, but I definitely remembered the word.

A couple of months later, Dr. James and my fellow classmates were gathered online for one of our final Spiritual Practitioner Studies classes. Everyone was filled with a mix of bliss, excitement, trepidation, anticipation along with some sadness knowing that our intensive two-year journey as a collective was coming to a close. As I gave the closing Spiritual Mind Treatment at the end of the class, it seemed only fitting that *intertwingle* should find its way into that closing prayer. When I finished, I remember Dr. James saying—with this lovely, quizzical smile on his face: "Lesia, I don't know if it's a real word or not, but I love that word you used, *intertwingle*."

"That's your word!" I replied with glee, reminding him and everyone in the class of that fateful flub during one of his Sunday talks just a couple of months before. Some people remembered, others did not. Regardless, that made-up word was still working its magic, further fortifying our beautiful collective bond that had been forged over the past two years of spiritual study and expansion of consciousness.

Since then, I have continued using this sublimely charming word because it conveys concepts and feelings that similar words like interconnect, intertwine, or interrelate just don't. Sure, it's made up, but so what? Weren't all words new words at some point? And please, if words like *irregardless* can make it into the dictionary because enough people chose not to use the correct, actual word, *regardless*, then I see no problem with choosing to use a made-up word and allowing it to develop and crystalize its own meaning along the way.

How many times have we struggled to find the perfect word or words to describe something? A feeling, an experience, a knowing? When it comes to describing truth, oneness, God, and consciousness—even Love—pretty much everything falls short. There is poetry. There is art. There is music. There is how we *feel* thanks to the creativity that is expressed and the imagination that is sparked through these various mediums.

For me, *Intertwinglement* (and its variations *Intertwingle*, *Intertwingling*, and so on) is not just a noun or a thing, it is a verb. It is a state of being. It is the ongoing, eternal, ever-expanding activity of the one Universal Energetic Flow that inspires, ignites, and interconnects everyone and everything. It is oneness expressing and being reflected through and as everyone and everything—*every* moment of *every* day. And because it is infinite in scope and creative by nature—representative of the Infinite Potentiality we innately are—it is nothing short of *Divine*.

Like everything, the concept of *Divine Intertwinglement* is so much more than those two words. It is the experience of what's happening when someone else's curiosity is aroused and their imagination is sparked when they hear and/or use that word. It is the connection I share with you, knowing these words I'm writing now will one day be read by you, forging an everlasting bond between you and me. It is the glimmer of a smile or a twinkle in the eye as someone says, "Intertwingle, I've never heard that word before. What does it mean...?" It is the delight in sharing the story of how the word came to be, and how the retelling of that story further intertwingles both teller and listener—*now and always.*

There's a beautiful imaginal concept in Buddhism called Indra's Net, which for me describes the profundity and sacredness—the divinity—of Intertwinglement. This net is made up of infinite, equally spaced knots, and like the Universe it represents, has no beginning and no end. At the centre of each knot rests a glimmering, shimmering jewel that radiates all the light of the Universe, and represents each being that is, was, and ever will be.

As the net gently moves and billows, these gems of various colours catch, refract, and reflect the light of the entire Universe in their own unique, luminescent ways, glimmering and shimmering throughout eternity. As they reflect, they are reflected. As they mirror, they too are mirrored. And even though there is no one gem that is the centre of the net, depending on how or from where a gem is being viewed, it can be seen as either the focal point or as the point from which the whole of the Universe is being viewed. No matter how the net is moving, every jewel is always interconnecting, interrelating, and interacting with every other jewel—individually and collectively. As every multifaceted jewel radiates its own unique version of the Universal Light of which it is made, the entire bejewelled net glimmers, shimmers, and shines that much more brilliantly as a whole.

Indra's Net is a brilliant, mystical, almost magical illustration of *Divine Intertwinglement*. It speaks to the inspiration, eternality, and sacredness of how we are all—as are the gems in Indra's Net—unique, original expressions of something greater than we. It also speaks to how fundamentally interconnected we all are. Even as unique, original beings, at our core, we are all the one Universal Energy that is the essence—the light—of everyone and everything.

Through Soul Excavation, we become aware of our individual light. The more we embrace and embody our own light, the more we discover how interconnected and intertwingled we are with everyone and everything. As we begin to embrace and embody the Divine Intertwinglement of this universal light, the more we realize how brilliantly we can glimmer, shimmer, and shine *together* as Infinite Creativity, Resilience, and Love.

Chapter 10

A New Foundation - The Embodiment of Creativity, Resilience, and Love

"You are a ruby encased in granite.
How long will you deceive Us with this outer show?
O friend, We can see the truth in your eyes!
So come, return to the root of the root
  of your own soul."

  – Rumi, "We Can See the Truth in Your Eyes"

As we've seen throughout the book, Soul Excavation is the mindful, messy, and dynamic work of digging through and unearthing the limiting thoughts, stories, and beliefs that keep us feeling stuck; revealing life's most extraordinary treasure—the Infinite Creativity, Resilience, and Love we truly are.

Throughout my life, there were several times I became aware of my Soul Excavation, with some of those experiences illustrated in this book. As I dug into, unearthed, and explored how life had gotten to be the way it was, at times I was able to experience something other than the pain, anger, and fear that had been the kaleidoscopic lens through which I viewed the world. During those times, I would catch a glimpse of understanding, compassion, and forgiveness—not only a different way of viewing the world, but a more vibrant and truthful way of living and a lighter way of being. However, it wasn't until my deliberate foray into spiritual/ consciousness studies that I opened the door to and became actively engaged in discovering and living from and as the Infinite Creativity, Resilience, and Love I truly am.

* * *

Transformation in Thought

I listen,
I breathe,
And with *gratitude* I receive
Spirit's *infinite possibilities.*

Always expanding,
Always flowing,
My indwelling spirit is my true knowing;
And I, the soul expression of flow and ease.

I *know,* and
I *trust,*
And with conviction, I must
Change my tendency, saying 'yes' always to love, abundance, and
   grace!

A New Foundation

Forever giving,
Forever receiving,
Guiding my thoughts to *what serves me best in believing*
I declare and treat *recognizing* my *unique expression of Source* from
a deep and sacred place…

For *all* that is great,
For *all* that is good,
Knowing only 1000% perfection—no would, could, or should
Only the *best* the Universe has to offer—that's what I *expect*!

From *conscious mind*
Into *subjective mind*,
There are so many delicious 'chocolate chips' to find
As the Law manifests my thoughts in form—*re-flect*!

I release,
I let go,
Embodying spirit, allowing flow
With all of its mind-blowing awesomeness—to *expand and create*
without strife.

And so it is,
It is done.
The Law is *always* at work, and *we are all Won*!
Like Ernest Holmes said, "Change your thinking. Change your
Life!"

I wrote and submitted the above poem as the final assignment
for my first Science of Mind class, Foundations for Better Living.
Although I had already spent many years of my adult life digging
into the stories and experiences of my past and how they'd

impacted my life so far, it wasn't until I began my spiritual studies in earnest that my mind was opened to a new way of thinking. This new way of thinking became the foundation for a new way of not only viewing the world, but of living in and creating my world.

The first chapter of this book on fear illustrates how the tenuous and volatile relationship with my dad ended up impacting every thought, decision, and subsequent relationship in my life. For decades, that fear was cultivated—unknowingly—by three deep-rooted beliefs: "You're not good enough," "You're not smart enough," and "You don't have what it takes." Because I wasn't aware of them, I had no idea how strong their influence was on how I viewed myself and the world. Instead, I felt like something was missing. I felt as if there were something inherently wrong with me—like I was broken.

The chapter on failure shows how that foundation of fear influenced every thought, decision, and action regarding the unfolding and subsequent closing of my bakery. With those three limiting beliefs running the show, the five and a half years of planning, opening, and then closing the bakery ended up being more about proving my dad wrong—that I *was* smart enough, I *was* good enough, and that I *did* have what it took—than it was about creating a successful, enjoyable, profitable business based on the bakery's mission of *"Delighting our clients by treating them, our ingredients, and our world with love and respect."* On the surface, it may have looked like we were steeped in our mission. Yet underneath that beautiful, lofty, compassionate ideal (for me, anyway) was that seemingly rock-solid foundation of fear that had become the springboard for failure—with my bakery and life in general.

By chapter three on faith, however, I'd already encountered the Science of Mind philosophy. The concepts of there being one power or energetic flow greater than what we appear to be, and that we are creators of our reality according to how we think and use our minds—ideas I'd been introduced to by the likes of Wayne Dyer, Bruce Lipton, and Louise Hay—were now being expanded upon as I consciously embarked upon my journey of exploration and discovery of self through spiritual/consciousness studies.

As a reminder, the three main tenets of the Science of Mind philosophy are:

- **There is only one thing going on.** Call it God, the Universe, Energy, Love, or the quantum field—whatever is meaningful for you. It is the very essence of everyone and everything. It is infinite in scope (boundless, limitless, eternal), and creative by nature (it's always shifting, changing, evolving, and expanding).

- **Everyone and everything is that one thing**—*in its entirety*. In other words, we are all walking, talking, living, breathing, unique, original expressions of that Infinite Creative Energy. This includes tangible things like people, places, and things. It also includes intangible things like thoughts, beliefs, and feelings. God or Energy is all there is. There is *nothing* that isn't God. There is *nothing* that isn't Energy.

- **We live according to spiritual and natural laws, with the main law being the Law of Cause and Effect.** From a scientific perspective, you kick a ball, it moves. You kick a wall, either the wall gets dented, or your foot breaks. From a spiritual perspective, what you think, believe, and feel becomes the foundation for your life experience.

191

Becoming aware of these teachings was one thing. Creating a life based on them was another. This teaching wasn't just about learning a new way of thinking. It was about embracing a new way of thinking in order to embody a new way of living. It was about a new way of being.

For me, these teachings provided an interpretation of God and faith that was very different from the one I'd grown up with. Instead of God being a power or superhuman-like entity that was separate from me, with heaven being an actual destination to reach when I died, I discovered that God was pure Energy. And because that Energy was the very essence of everyone and everything, I too was this Energy—infinite in scope, and creative by nature. It meant I wasn't just a part of God, but that I was all of God—*to the degree I identified (or believed) as such.*

From that first Foundations for Better Living class, I felt so liberated and empowered to learn that I was more powerful than anything I'd ever thought, believed, felt, or experienced. I was so excited to realize I could actually create a different life experience just by using my mind differently. Fast-forward five years later, after a year of Advanced Consciousness Studies and our plunge into the quantum sea of no time or space and infinite possibilities, my understanding of God and faith has deepened and expanded even further.

Let's go over some of the fundamental takeaways of quantum physics:

- **The quantum field is the realm of infinite potentiality and is not bound by time or space.** Everything in the quantum field exists as a wave of possibility or a particle of actuality. When we choose a wave of possibility by putting our attention on it (when we think), that wave immediately changes into its actualized counterpart (it becomes a thing). This happens *instantaneously*, without anyone or anything having to wait or travel anywhere for that change to happen. Based on our tendency of thought (our habitual thinking patterns) and our worldview (is the world a safe and friendly place or is it a threatening and horrible place?), our choices are shaped into what we end up experiencing.

- **Everyone creates their reality.** There is no separate reality occurring outside of what we experience as our reality, even though the things and circumstances of life make a very convincing argument otherwise. This means that even if we appear to be having a collective experience with others, every individual experience is different because everyone is creating their version of the agreed-upon collective reality. Because everyone has their habitual thought patterns and worldview, two people can interpret or perceive the "same" experience in very different ways.

- **There are infinite realities that can be potentially experienced at any given time.** The quantum field is filled with infinite possibilities, and because it is not bound by time or space, all possible realities—past, present, and future (or rather our perception of past, present, and future)—are occurring *simultaneously*. This means any of them can be experienced *in the present moment*. Is it magic? Not really, even though it might feel like it. Is it easy? Not necessarily, but it can be. Can anyone do it? 100%! The more we consciously practice focusing our attention on what's possible, rather than what's probable (based on our habitual thought patterns and existing worldview), the more we create new trajectories for us to travel—*as we're creating them*. This is how the probable becomes the inevitable! It's the alchemical magic of mysticism and the wonder of science coming together as the exciting, exhilarating practice of living from the unknown of infinite possibilities.

- **Even though it may appear to be, reality is not constant.** The Universe is refreshing and rebooting itself anew—*as are we*—every moment of every day. Every single now moment is a brand-spankin'-new opportunity of life and living!

The further I delved into the quantum realm, the less I understood. The less I understood, the more uncomfortable I became. The more uncomfortable I became, the more I kicked and screamed. Eventually, I kicked and screamed myself right out of my comfort zone and into a new world of infinite possibilities.

In this new world, nothing was set in stone. In this new world, the only reality happening was the one I was creating. In this new world of infinite possibilities, absolutely nothing was static, and the Universe was constantly creating itself anew. The more I settled into this new world beyond time and space, the more I realized how Infinitely powerful I truly am.

There was also another level to this new worldview. Thanks to my Advanced Consciousness Studies class experience and our foray into the quantum realm where time and space weren't an issue, I discovered that I could draw from "future" realities or visit "past" realities as I saw fit. By placing my attention on those alternate realities, the trajectory or path of that reality would instantaneously change. By drawing on emotion and enthusiasm from or infusing emotion into these alternate realities—whether seemingly past or future—I could instantly change my present reality. In turn, my changed present reality would then shape the alternate realities associated with those changed trajectories or paths.

What I could also do, though—which was and still feels astounding in an otherworldly kind of way—is let go of the limiting belief of time as I'd come to understand it.

The spiritual principle in play here is that "Time expands to meet my needs." In letting go of the notion that time is an actual thing that unfolds in one direction like a straight line, I could visit my younger self and fundamentally change my relationship to the three main limiting beliefs that had shaped most of my life experience. In providing my younger self with the tender, loving-kindness we are all deserving of just because we are, that shift in empowerment would then alter the foundation of my younger self, which was eventually shaped by the innate truth that I am a unique, original expression of Infinite Creativity, Resilience, and Love. That foundational shift in perspective for my younger self would then simultaneously empower my present self, rooting me more firmly in the knowing and the faith that I am that same Infinite Creativity, Resilience, and Love—*right here, right now, and always.*

But wait, there's more.

The real nugget in all of this is that all of it—every single thought, belief, feeling, and experience—has been a *projection* of my mind.

This includes my relationship with my dad—then and now. It includes everything that unfolded during the planning, opening, and subsequent closing of my bakery. And it includes every aspect of our cross-country move experience.

Sure, it may seem like others were involved in what I experienced or that there is a reality that would keep plugging along even if I were to be plucked out of it. However, remember, according to quantum physics, there is no separately occurring reality outside of ourselves. *We*—no one else—create our reality. Even when there is an agreed-upon seemingly collective experience, everyone's perception of that experience is different based on their own tendency of thought and worldview. As this new realization sinks in, *everything* changes.

Which brings me back to my poem of five years ago.

When I look at that poem today, I definitely honoured the assignment. It's filled with a myriad of Science of Mind terms, ideas, and concepts—even to the point of instruction—the majority of which still ring true for me today. Even the title and last line of the poem speak to the transformation we are all capable of experiencing according to how we think and use our minds.

Today, that poem is also an amazing reminder of how much I've grown and evolved over the past five years and throughout my lifetime, *period*. Having been written at the beginning of my spiritual/consciousness studies and Soul Excavation process, this poem is a testament to the spiritual lens through which I was learning to view the world then. It is also a tribute to the quantum lens through which I endeavour to view the world now.

I understand that I am always creating my reality based on how I use my mind and what I am choosing to focus on. I realize that my reality is mine and that I—no one else—am ultimately responsible for my life experience.

I *know*, and
I *trust*,
And with conviction, I must
Change my tendency, saying 'yes' always to love, abundance, and
grace!

Forever giving,
Forever receiving,
Guiding my thoughts to *what serves me best in believing*
I declare and treat *recognizing* my *unique expression of Source* from
a deep and sacred place...

This steadfast, unwavering faith of *knowing* Who and What I am is the new foundation from which I live my life. Instead of living life from the limitations of pain, anger, and fear, I live from a more expanded awareness of understanding, compassion, and loving-kindness—for everyone and everything. Because of this new foundation, I now choose to view my relationship with my dad through a more compassionate and forgiving lens—for him and for me. I choose to see the extraordinary opportunities for growth and expansion that resulted during the operation and closure of my bakery. I choose to view every challenge faced during our cross-country move as a new opportunity to return to the "root of the root" of my soul.

"There is always more, and I am always more than..." I am not my thoughts, beliefs, feelings, or experiences. I am the ruby in Rumi's poem, and I choose to no longer remain encased in granite.

I am Infinite Creativity, Resilience, and Love. And as such, I am infinitely more powerful, creative, and resilient than anything I could ever think, believe, feel, or experience—*now and always.*

Section 4

The Excavation Continues

"There are two aspects of life: the first is that man is tuned by his surroundings, and the second is that man can tune himself in spite of his surroundings."

– Hazrat Inayat Khan

I began this book by telling you about my dad. I shared how when I was little, I thought he was the smartest, most handsome, charming, funny, charismatic man around and that I wanted to be just like him when I grew up. I also talked about our tenuous relationship, which was filled with physical, emotional, and mental abuse. I talked about how because of that abuse, I spent most of my life living from a foundation of fear, mired in failure, with little faith in anyone or anything including myself.

I also talked about my ever-evolving relationship with God. I conveyed how when I was a little girl, I loved being Ukrainian Catholic. The culture, artistry, and ritual of church, along with the music of the Divine Liturgy resonated so profoundly with me, that when I grew up, I wanted to become a Ukrainian Catholic priest. However, once I learned that could never happen because I was a girl, that, along with other circumstances, eventually led me to question and abandon the concepts of God and faith— period. As a result, for many years of my young adult life, I found myself faithless, choosing to believe there was no God.

Today, after several years of the mindful, messy, and dynamic work of Soul Excavation, I see the parallels of those two seemingly separate relationships. I see how I idolized and revered both my dad and God, and how I wanted to "be" just like each of them when I grew up. I wanted to be my dad because he was so talented and amazing and could make people feel great with his presence. I wanted to be a Ukrainian Catholic priest because that meant serving God, which also meant helping people to feel great (with *His* presence).

I also see the evolution of both relationships. Over time, what began as love and worship turned to questioning and eventually denial. Just as I'd gotten out from under my dad's roof around the age of eighteen, I had also chosen to get out from under God's.

The problem was, though, when it comes to parents and God, out of sight is not necessarily out of mind. So, for years, even though my dad may not have been physically present in my life, he still took up valuable space in my mind. And for years, even though I had decided God didn't exist, I'd still find myself plagued or at the very least mystified, with who I was and what my purpose in life might be. When it came to both my dad and God, I'd also find myself explaining to various family, friends, and community members why when both seemed to exist, neither was an active part of my life.

* * *

At the end of our second-to-last Advanced Consciousness Studies class, Dr. James gave us our final assignment. We were asked to give a five-minute presentation during our final class on what the year's forty-week-long experience had meant to us.

As I closed my laptop, I felt a surge of sadness knowing that the collective class experience of the past year was coming to an end. Even though we still had one more class to go, I was already missing my fellow classmates. Even though I'd felt bogged down with reading and writing all year long, I suddenly found myself wondering what I'd do with all those extra hours in the week and on Thursday evenings. Without knowing what next year's accelerated ministerial program would be like—or if it would even happen—I wondered what the next level of spiritual/consciousness studies would entail. I wondered how my studies would further activate my ongoing Soul Excavation as my exploration into and discovery of self continued to inform my ongoing studies.

I passed the living room window on the west side of the house and marvelled at how light blue the sky still was at 10:15 at night. Then, as I walked into the kitchen to look out the east facing wall of windows, I stopped dead in my tracks.

At the time, we lived on the second floor of a house, and our wall of windows in the kitchen looked out onto a big backyard. Bordering the backyard was a tall grove of trees, with acres and acres of farmland on the other side. Beyond that expanse of farmland was the ocean, and then the mountains. Because there were no tall buildings, the sky above was vast.

That night, as I looked out of the kitchen windows, amazed at how dark it was on this side of the sky, I saw a bright, golden, orangey glow peaking its way through the treetops at the end of our yard. Having watched numerous moonrises over the years, I knew it'd only take a few minutes before the full body of the moon would emerge above the treeline.

I ran to get Mylana—who was still awake—and even woke up Glenn—who'd been sound asleep for some time—to view this exquisite moon as it rose its way up into the night sky. I wanted someone else to experience this extraordinary event with me.

When I got back not even a minute later, about half of the moon was visible. It was so plump and round, and its glow spilled out into the night sky. I wanted to get a better view, so I grabbed and climbed up a step ladder to see above the treetops.

As the moon continued to rise, I looked up and saw long feathery clouds strewn across the night sky, with the tips of the clouds appearing to have been dipped in pink. Only one star was visible. And on the other side of the house, the sky still looked a periwinkle blue.

I gazed at the moon, and that's when it hit me. There, on a step ladder on our deck, in the middle of a sizzling-hot summer night, I saw the moon slowly rising while also being lifted up by the sky. As the light of the moon spilled out into the night, there was no end to the moon or beginning to the sky. Same with the clouds. They hung in the air while being cradled by the breeze. And the stars that were beginning to twinkle—almost as if they were being blinked into existence—were a reflection and extension of the brilliant luminescence radiating from the enormous grapefruit moon in the sky.

As I gazed at all of this Divine Intertwinglement in action, I felt it all in *every* cell of my body. As I felt it all, I felt every single classmate *with me*.

I felt their love, their wisdom, their curiosity, and their joy. I knew that each breath I was taking was also theirs, and that they were a reflection of me and I of them. I also knew we were all unique, original expressions of the same Energy that shone the moon and held it in the sky, that painted the wispy ends of the feather clouds, that illuminated each twinkling star throughout the night.

I knew there and then that, in creating my class experience of the past forty weeks, I'd also created a community where I belonged. I had created—kicking and screaming for most of the time—a community that had not only challenged my understanding of Who and What I am, but also of what I can *become*. And now—thanks to our plunge into the quantum sea—the endless possibilities and infinite potentiality of that becoming had also led me to a deeper understanding of my relationship with my dad and of God.

Tears of love, joy, and gratitude filled my eyes and blew open my heart. I watched the moon for several minutes longer, silently basking in the profundity of the experience of belonging, of oneness.

This profound experience of oneness has also enabled me to view, revisit, and recreate my relationship with my dad in a new light. Instead of looking at it from a "he did this," "I did that," or "that's what happened" viewpoint, I now see that *everything* that transpired between me and my dad (from my perspective anyway) had everything to do with how I saw my dad, and not Who and What he really is. How I saw my dad also had everything to do with how I viewed myself, and not Who and What I really am.

Does this mean there was no violence or trauma? No. Does it mean all the pain, anger, and fear I experienced just gets neatly put away in a box and shoved to the back of the closet of ignorance and bliss? Again, no.

It means that, now that I know what I know, I can't go back and *unknow* it. Now that I know I am divinely intertwingled with everyone and everything—through time, space, and beyond—I am a reflection of my dad and he of me. And both of us are reflections of God.

Seven years ago, in the days leading up to his death, my dad kept repeating the phrase, "God is Love." Even though at the time the phrase and the word "God" got under my skin, I'd repeat those words back to him because I could see that they brought him great comfort and peace of mind.

Today, as I continue my spiritual/consciousness studies and Soul Excavation—choosing to tune myself *in spite of my surroundings*—I am grateful for my dad and for every aspect of our relationship. And, knowing that God is Infinite Potentiality not bound by time or space, I know and feel with all my heart my dad is listening when I say, "God is Love, and Love is all there is. It is Who and What I am. It is Who and What you are. Thank you, God. I love you."

* * *

"From then on, the boy understood his heart. He asked it, please, never to stop speaking to him. He asked that, when he wandered far from his dreams, his heart press him and sound the alarm. The boy swore that, every time he heard the alarm, he would heed this message."

– Paulo Coelho, *The Alchemist*

Just over a year ago, I discovered and crafted my "Why" (à la Simon Sinek): *"To empower the conscious awakening of humanity so that together, we can cultivate a global community founded in Love."* As I continue to actively engage in my conscious awakening through ongoing spiritual/consciousness studies and ever-deepening

Soul Excavation, I am so grateful to keep connecting, engaging, and intertwingling with people of different faiths and beliefs from all over the world, as together, we cultivate a global community founded in Love.

More importantly, I have come to realize that the more we embody the Infinite Creativity, Resilience, and Love we are at our core—*individually and collectively*—the better we are able to cultivate a global community founded in Love—*regardless* of what is going on. As we continue to live from and as that Love, we actively immerse ourselves in the dreams of our heart and allow our Soul to start singing. The more we actively tune into the extraordinary, vibrant, fulfilling life that is ours to live, the more we unearth the brilliance, mystery, and purpose of Soul that is ours to discover.

Bibliography

Brown, Lesley. *The New Shorter Oxford English Dictionary.* 1993 ed. New York: Oxford University Press, 1993.

Coelho, Paulo. *The Alchemist.* 25th Ann. ed. New York: HarperOne, 2014.

Gilbert, Elizabeth. *Big Magic: Creative Living Beyond Fear.* New York: Riverhead Books, 2015.

Holmes, Ernest. *The Science of Mind: A Philosophy, A Faith, A Way of Life.* Def ed. New York: TarcherPerigee, 2012.

Khan, Hazrat Inayat. *Sayings.* New York: Sufi Order Publications, 1978.

Khan, Hazrat Inayat. *Vol. 2, The Mysticism and Sound of Music.* New ed. India: Motilal Banarsidass Publishing House, 2009.

Ladinsky, Daniel. *A Year with Hafiz: Daily Contemplations.* New York: Penguin Books (USA), 2011.

Levy, Paul. *The Quantum Revelation: A Radical Synthesis of Science and Spirituality.* 1st ed. New York: SelectBooks, 2018.

Moore, Thomas. *Care of the Soul: A Guide for Cultivating Depth and Sacredness in Everyday life.* 25th Ann. ed. New York: Harper Perennial, 1992.

Morter, Dr. Sue. *The Energy Codes: The 7-Step System to Awaken Your Spirit, Heal Your Body, and Live Your Best Life.* 1st ed. New York: Atria Books, 2019.

Nemeth, Maria, Ph.D. *The Energy of Money: A Spiritual Guide to Personal and Financial Fulfilment.* 1st ed. New York: Ballantine Wellspring, 1999.

Nepo, Mark. *Seven Thousand Ways to Listen: Staying Close to What Is Sacred.* 1st ed. New York: Atria Books, 2013.

Star, Jonathan. Rumi: *In the Arms of the Beloved.* New York: Tarcher Cornerstone, 1997.

Tolle, Eckhart. *A New Earth: Awakening to Your Life's Purpose.* London: Plume, 2006.

Gratitude

I am grateful for it all—the sweet, the sour, and everything in between. There are, however, certain people to whom I feel deeply indebted, knowing their contributions were integral, even essential in helping this exploration and discovery—this labour of self-love—to be written and published as a book. Celebrating them here is but a tiny way of saying thank you.

To Karen Strauss, Sara Foley, Karina Cooke, and the entire Hybrid Global Publishing Team—I am forever grateful for your guidance, support, patience, expertise, flexibility, and gentle nudges along the way. Every creative collaboration was brilliantly matched and the steep learning curve notwithstanding the entire publishing process an absolute thrill.

To my developmental editor, now friend, Joy Stocke—there are no words to express my gratitude for your wisdom, talent, enthusiasm, and support. You gave me the tools to be a better writer. Your four-week crash course in creative writing helped me to sculpt a better book. "Show don't tell" is now forever etched in my mind—a new groove, mantra, and activational reminder to paint an imaginal picture, inviting the reader to experience the story rather than simply read about it.

To my first-round proofers and editors—Dale, Glenn, Emily, Joselito, and Virginia—I am eternally grateful for your time, enthusiasm, love, and support. Your candid and creative suggestions, questions, and insights inspired me to submit a readable, understandable, relatable, and well-organized first draft for my degree.

To my accountability partner, classmate, and fellow Mystical Maven, Lori—I am infinitely grateful for your wisdom, tenacity, creativity, enthusiasm, inspired poetic pivot, and love, and for giving me that one anecdotal gem—along with so many other nuggets of wisdom—to keep both of us on track as we opened up to and unleashed creativity with our respective final assignments.

To my friend Jane—thank you for your love and support. Your generosity, faith, trust, and belief in me allowed me to publish this book in the way I envisioned.

To my friend Phyllis (a.k.a. BFF)—your kindness, generosity, enthusiasm, love, laughter, and support were integral to keeping me grounded during times of upheaval throughout the writing and editing process.

To photographer extraordinaire, creative genius, and friend Linda—thank you for capturing my true essence "on film," and for all of our creative collaborations so far.

To my mom, Khrystia, daughter, Mylana, sister, Larissa, Aunt Vera; to my friends Laura, Seema, and Janet; and to all of the other brilliant, powerful, creative, kind, loving, inspirational, women who find the sacred in the mundane, who reveal the extraordinary in the ordinary, who push themselves to be a better, more inspired, engaging, fulfilled version of who they are in this moment—you continue to show time and again you are infinitely more powerful, creative, and resilient than anything you could ever think, believe, or feel, than anything you could ever experience. I love you; I appreciate you; and I'm forever grateful for your time and presence in my life.

To my Baba Stepha—I see your hands in mine. I feel your love, kindness, and fortitude in your recipes and every bread, doughnut, pastry, and cake I create. *Diakuiu, bab.*

To my beloved LPK's Culinary Groove staff—I appreciate you more than you will ever know. I celebrate what each one of you has and continues to become. You anchored me in creativity, celebration, and fortitude during some of the most challenging times of my life. You hold a very special place in my heart, and I continue to cherish the laughter, joy, enthusiasm, care, dancing, singing, patience, creativity, commitment, and friendship that were key to the LPK's mission of "Delighting our clients by threating them, our ingredients, and our world with love and respect."

To my clients—thank you for your courage, vulnerability, and candor. Thank you for trusting me to support and hold a safe and sacred space for you as you feel the feels, cry the tears, and navigate the questions, confusion, and frustration that arise while digging into and exploring the depths of your soul. Thank you for teaching, expanding, and healing me along the way. Thank you for the gift of celebrating with you as you reveal the Infinite Creativity, Resilience, and Love you truly are—that you've been all along.

To my prayer partners, past and present—Aimee, Bonnie, Corrine, Dale, Emily, Gail, Joselito, Karen, Kirby, Linda, and Liza—thank you for your powerful presence, your wisdom, and love. I am grateful you've been able to know for me when I've not been able to know for myself. Thank you for every brilliant, inspirational, activational reminder that I am the Infinite Expanse of the Universe in action, capable of being and doing anything I set my mind to.

To my Spiritual Practitioner Studies classmates and members of the "Care of the Soil" study group—I am grateful for your friendship, kinship, curiosity, and the expansive, intimate, life-altering journey we've travelled and shared so far.

To my Advanced Consciousness Studies classmates—Even if it's all made up and there are no words, I love and am infinitely grateful for every single one of you. As I write, I feel the magic, mysticism, and divine intertwinglement of that moonrise and the mind-bending, gut-wrenching, foundation-shattering, heart-opening, forty-week exploration into consciousness that our collective birthed together. You will forever be my grapefruit moon.

To the Centre of Love, Global Truth Center Los Angeles, Emerson Theological Institute, Unity Spiritual Community of Victoria, CSL Victoria, and Global Truth Centre Toronto—thank you for the space, means, and ongoing opportunity to dig into, unearth, explore, challenge, and continually question what is mine to do, who is mine to be, and how is mine to show up in this world.

To you, dear reader—thank you for your curiosity and willingness to explore. May you find something of value within these stories that helps you to let go of the limiting thoughts, stories, and beliefs that have kept you feeling stuck until now. May some word, idea, or turn of phrase reveal a gem of insight or nugget of wisdom so that you can begin to understand that just because life has been a certain way until now, doesn't mean it has to be that way going forward.

Lastly, I am eternally grateful to the three men in my life who have taught me the most about Love. I am eternally grateful to my dad who challenged me—kicking and screaming—into questioning the meaning of Love. I am grateful to my teacher, Dr. James Mellon, who challenged and continues to challenge me—often kicking and screaming—to embrace and more fully embody the "Greatness on Demand" and Love that I am. Most of all, I am grateful to my husband, (the L.O.M.L.) Glenn, who is the embodiment of kindness, compassion, curiosity, and patience as we continually challenge each other to live more fully from and as the Love we both are. *Honeybunch, I umpsquelve you.*

For everything that has already made its way forward and for everything that is yet to come, I remain forever grateful.

With Infinite Love and Gratitude,

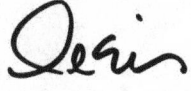

About the Author

Lesia Kohut is a speaker, podcaster, activist, and coach. She holds a bachelor's degree in Advanced Consciousness Studies and is a Religious Science Practitioner and Integrative Nutrition Health Coach.

Through the work of Soul Excavation, Lesia helps busy, open-minded professionals get to the root cause of their problems so that they can make better decisions, be more successful, and achieve desired goals and intentions in their relationships, finances, career, and health. Her podcast, "Who Do You *Think* You Are?" is available on YouTube and major podcast platforms.

She lives, breathes, works, and plays with her husband, community, and cat Mercury on Vancouver Island. To connect with Lesia please visit www.lesia@lesiakohut.com.

Soul Excavation: An Exploration and Discovery of Self Through Fear, Failure, and Quantum Physics is her first book.

CPSIA information can be obtained
at www.ICGtesting.com
Printed in the USA
BVHW050820271122
652785BV00006B/9

9 781957 013251